THE
STRESS
MANAGEMENT
HANDBOOK

THE NEW HOPE STRESS MANAGEMENT
HANDBOOK

....

A Practical Guide to Staying Calm, Keeping Cool, and Avoiding Blow-Ups

....

EVA SELHUB, MD

Skyhorse Publishing

Skyhorse Publishing books may be purchased in bulk at special discounts for sales promotion, corporate gifts, fund-raising, or educational purposes. Special editions can also be created to specifications. For details, contact the Special Sales Department, Skyhorse Publishing, 307 West 36th Street, 11th Floor, New York, NY 10018 or info@ skyhorsepublishing.com.

Skyhorse® and Skyhorse Publishing® are registered trademarks of Skyhorse Publishing, Inc.®, a Delaware corporation.

Visit our website at www.skyhorsepublishing.com.

10 9 8 7 6 5 4 3 2 1

Library of Congress Cataloging-in-Publication Data is available on file.

Cover design by Abigail Gehring
Cover illustration by iStockphoto

Print ISBN: 978-1-5107-3050-2
Ebook ISBN: 978-1-5107-3051-9

Printed in China

*I lovingly dedicate this book to my parents,
my beacons of love,
Jacob and Shirley Selhub.*

Contents

· ·

Introduction
Why Stress Is Normal

·····················

"The truth will set you free, but first it will piss you off."

—Gloria Steinhem

In the early years of my spiritual studies, I truly believed that my job as a spiritual guide and rational physician was to stay clearheaded, loving, and peaceful. For me, showing anger was simply a no-no. The problem was that I failed quite miserably and often, especially while driving in my hometown of Boston.

On one such occasion, while driving home from work, another driver pulled in ahead of my car without warning, causing me to step on my breaks suddenly. I, of course, honked my horn several times and in response, the driver flipped me the bird. Obscenities flew out of my mouth. How dare he throw an offensive gesture at me when he was in the wrong! How dare he risk my life! I fumed.

Within a few minutes of blowing up, I started to feel guilty. I thought to myself, *How could you do that? You are a spiritual person and a meditator and you just lost it. Good people don't swear at other people. The Dalai Lama never would have behaved this way!* It was the last line about the Dalai Lama that stopped me in my ranting and raving tracks. I actually started laughing as my thoughts switched to, *Who are you comparing yourself to exactly? Not only are you not his Holiness, but you have no desire to be him either. In addition, the Dalai Lama doesn't drive. He has drivers. He, therefore, does not have to deal with crazy drivers.* Lightening up with laughter also allowed me to take a momentary step back from my anger and observe the statement *Good people don't swear at other people.* It made me question myself: *What does that mean? If I swear and act human, I am not good? Is that even true?*

My inner dialogue had given me pause. It led me to realize that my anger, the emotion itself, was actually appropriate for the circumstance. My life had been put in danger, and I was made to feel insignificant and disregarded. What may not have been so appropriate was the intensity and the way I expressed my anger, which did little good for me or anyone else. It certainly did not help me feel any better, although temporarily the cursing did enable me to release some of my pent-up energy.

So I asked myself why. Why did I react the way I did, and was it possible to react differently? Was it possible for me to maintain a sense of peace and calm, despite feeling disrespected? And did my reaction have anything to do with me judging myself as not being "good," or somehow "bad?"

When I got home, I sat quietly, meditated, and reflected. I thought about being cut off in traffic and connected with the feelings of being disrespected, insignificant, invisible, not good, and not enough. When I tapped into these negative feelings, I realized they were not new to me. I had felt this way countless times before. Each of these negative experiences, in turn, gave evidence to my negative self-image.

I understood then that the situation itself didn't make me feel these feelings but rather brought them out in me; that my history of having had similar hurtful experiences had caused me to feel invisible or unworthy in one shape or form and that these pre-existing hurts or wounds were causing me to react when provoked. In other words, I realized that my anger may have been appropriate given the situation, but the emotional outburst was a product of my deep hurts—deep hurts within me that not only caused me to overreact with anger, but also provided me with ongoing evidence that I was insignificant or not good enough.

I understood that as long as I lived my life looking through a lens that led me to see myself as not enough, there would be a higher chance of me getting triggered and angered by life events. If I was attacking me, it would take very little to push me overboard into believing that someone else or the world was attacking me. I also realized that there were many times that I did not look through such a negative lens; the times I did look through this negative lens were when I was depleted, tired, stressed, or unhappy.

Put yourself in this scenario: If you are in a good mood and reading your book and I tap you on the shoulder to get your attention, it may annoy you slightly. But if I tap you on the shoulder where you happen to have a gaping wound festering, you would scream high holy murder and likely slap my hand. You are already in pain and having a hard time concentrating, and here I come, totally oblivious to your discomfort, and hurt you. You would be outraged and act out. You might also then feel guilty or ashamed for hitting me once you realize that I was just trying to get your attention and meant no harm. If the wound did not already exist, would you not have simply been annoyed with my mindless behavior? Would you have gotten so angry?

Probably not.

The Hurt Can Heal

My take-home message was that if I wanted to be able to stay blissful despite distress, I was going to have to be able to heal my old hurts. As long as these hurts were alive and present, situations could trigger a reaction that would always bypass my logical brain and ultimately generate a stress reaction infused with rage or fear.

If I wanted to live my life happily, not only was I going to have to do something about these wounds, but I had to work on feeling more valued within myself, know I was inherently "good," and take better care of myself in every possible way—through nurturing my body and mind with healthy eating, sleeping, exercising, and thinking more loving thoughts toward myself. The more valued I felt, the less seriously I would need to take myself and most things in life, as I wouldn't feel threatened.

That day, I began creating techniques and healing processes that would soothe the hurt, create a sense of calm and peace, and ignite the feeling of being valued rather than the feeling of being disrespected or invisible. I found that the more I practiced these techniques, the calmer I became as a person. Better yet, I found that if I was upset, I could calm myself enough to use the tension or stress that I was feeling to motivate positive rather than hurtful action.

I ultimately realized that I had a choice: I could choose to be a victim of my past and my life and to continue living my life looking through a lens of negativity, feel stressed and miserable, or choose to be a victor and live my life looking through a lens of joy.

The Choice to Know Your Value

You have a choice of whether or not you blow up or bliss out, whether you let your stress control you and weaken you or use it to become more powerful and happy. It is up to you to decide if you want to seek value outside of yourself and continuously feel disappointed and lacking, or work toward knowing your own value from within. It is up to you to decide if you want to be stuck waiting for happiness to come or choose to be happy because, ultimately, using stress to your advantage, you can be.

Know that stress itself is natural and necessary in that it motivates you to take action when some sort of threat to your state of balance is present. The problem is that when stress triggers negative emotions, the negative emotions can overwhelm you and short-circuit your brain and your higher intellectual reasoning, causing you to fall into behaviors that are often hurtful to others or to yourself. The deeper your hurts, the stronger your negative emotions, and the bigger the negative reaction will be. Trying to stop the reaction is often close to impossible, like trying to stop a shiver when it is cold outside.

What if you were to start looking at stress differently? What if you were to realize that any time you are feeling stressed or distressed, which is stress associated with a negative emotion, you are actually receiving a warning signal that you are running on empty and you need to refuel?

If you were to start approaching distress differently, by reacting less strongly or not at all for that matter, you would give yourself the opportunity to heal any part of you that feels broken. The less broken you then feel, the more whole you become. The more whole you are, the less triggered and distressed you will be. You have more balance within yourself and your life. You feel good, and inevitably, you are a lot happier. A happier and more whole you is a more successful you.

In Search of Happy

Though most people claim they want to be healthy, the truth is, everyone just wants to be happy. Everyone wants to feel good. The problem is that most people believe that happiness comes from outside factors.

Why does this happen? Because inherently, people do not possess a core belief that they are enough and have the ability to create happy with or without the things they seek. They constantly look outside of themselves for happiness—looking for more wealth, a perfect partner, a perfect family, and so forth—not realizing that nothing will ever be enough and no one and nothing can be exactly what they need them to be. The harder they seek, the more disappointed they become, and the harder it seems to achieve happiness.

Think about your own life. Perhaps you are married and you are constantly angry with your spouse for not understanding you or for simply not taking out the trash. Perhaps you are single and you believe that if only you had a partner, you would be happy. Or maybe you think you will be happier if you had more money, a different president, a new boss, or a world where everyone was pleasant and courteous. Whatever it is you seek, you don't have it now, which makes you feel lacking and will exist forever feeling you are not enough. Fast forward to everyday life, and someone cuts you off in traffic, is rude to you on the phone, is taking too long in the checkout line, or just isn't listening to you when you are talking, or . . . *boom!* You lose it. Surprised?

Is it surprising that you blow up when life throws you a curveball when you are already feeling out of balance and unhappy?

Freedom Is Bliss

The key is to find what you are seeking within yourself, rather than outside of yourself, and to fix the "not enough" syndrome. The more whole and balanced you are, the less triggered you will be, and the more likely you will find your bliss.

Do you remember a time when you felt bliss? All you need to do is think back to a time when you felt free, without worries, on top of the world, happy, at peace. Maybe you were on vacation. Or maybe you were five years old playing in the mud. Or perhaps it was the moment you fell in love. Bliss. You have felt it before. You know you have. And since you have felt it before, it is definitely possible to feel it again.

The path to attaining bliss is freedom. I am not referring to the freedom that comes in the form of no responsibility to others or to yourself, but the freedom that comes from not being attached—to things, to people, to your emotions, or to your suffering. This kind of freedom involves letting go of the things, beliefs, or ideas you think determine your value and your happiness. It's the sort of freedom you get when you feel good because you choose to, not because you are waiting for something or someone else to make it so. When you are not attached to your expectations, negative stories, or beliefs about how life is supposed to be, you get freedom. With this freedom, you get happiness.

Happiness lies in your ability to focus on feeling good and feeling bliss in ways that you create yourself. This is not to say that the aim is for you to deny or squelch other feelings; rather, the goal is for you to learn to be unattached to negative feelings and suffering, to be less controlled by them so that you can heal and feel free. When you feel free, negative people and situations simply don't bother you as much.

This book will teach specific tools to help you hone in on the cause of your distress and to release it and to discover ways you can create your own happiness. You will be shown ways to nurture yourself, build your support framework, and feel stronger and more powerful. Through the framework of this easy and practical guide to stress management, you will learn that even in the midst of a dark abyss, you can find your bliss.

Chapter 1
Understand the Stress Response
& Negative Emotions

....

"Letting go gives us freedom, and freedom is the only condition for happiness. If, in our heart, we still cling to anything—anger, anxiety, or possessions—we cannot be free."

—Thich Nhat Hanh, *The Heart of the Buddha's Teaching:*
Transforming Suffering into Peace, Joy, and Liberation

After practicing medicine for over twenty-five years, I have come to believe that the majority of the people on this earth live their life in fear of dying, of not being important, or of not being truly loved, prohibiting their ability to live a full and beautiful life. The reason most people live in fear of death is that they don't know or believe they are truly loved or loveable, or they don't know their own value. When people feel truly loved, when they understand their inherent value, worth, or importance, they are likely to care for themselves and their environment, experience fewer health problems, feel less psychologically and emotionally upset, and ultimately, have less distress, fear, or rage.

Think about this: If you truly loved yourself and knew your worth, would you not do everything in your power to nurture your body, your mind, your soul, and your spirit? If you nurtured yourself so much that you felt valued and overflowing with love, would you not be happy, and would you then be less easily insulted or even care less if someone else paid you no mind or insulted you?

Of course you would!

You have the ability to be truly happy, and that ability lies in your very own body.

You have a magnificent body made of trillions of cells, some of them strong, some of them weak. No matter their strength, these cells help one another, protecting one another from harm and aligning together to give you a chance to have a fabulous life on this earth. When these cells are not properly nurtured, taken care of, or supported, they cannot then fully support you to live and shine, to be happy and successful.

The beauty of your body is that it is always letting you know when it is in need, when it desires help or change from you. The signals come in the form of sensations like hunger or fatigue, a cough, a sense of discomfort, or a negative emotion or thought. These signals tell you when you are in stress or when you are safe, when you are out of balance or in balance, when you are in a state of unrest or a state of peace and love. The food you eat, the people you spend time with, the movements you make, the thoughts you uphold or the words you speak—all affect each one of your cells positively or negatively. In turn, these cells let you know if your actions are helping you thrive or dive.

If you were to pay attention, love yourself, and truly want to be and stay happy, you would heed your body's signals and avoid behaviors and actions that cause you to dive and uphold only those that help you thrive.

You have a choice. You have a choice every day and every moment of your life of whether or not you want to nurture your body and your Self or hurt it. The less you hurt yourself, the less the world can truly hurt you.

You have a choice of how you are going to view your life—in gratitude of having experiences that help you discover your true Self so that you can live life in the full beauty of your Self, or in remorse of never having or being enough so that you live your life feeling like a victim of your circumstances.

You have a choice to believe in the greatness of your Self that cannot be deflated by another, or you can believe that your Self is helpless and that you will only be great if you get recognized or valued by another.

If your choice is happy, all you really need to do is start paying attention to your body's signals.

Understanding Stress

Your body talks to you in the form of stress. Stress is the reason we procreate, innovate, run marathons, and get promotions. It is how we get out of bed in the morning and why we are motivated to put food on the table. When something within us wants change, we are driven to make it happen. That want for change is motivated by stress. Feeling tired? Stress. Feeling hungry? Stress. Low blood pressure? Stress again.

Stress is not necessarily bad. You need it to help you live, adapt, and survive. Stress motivates us to climb mountains or to innovate and find new ways to get more comfortable or to get somewhere faster.

What is stress exactly?

Stress is defined as any challenge to the balance (also known as homeostasis) of the body. Challenges can range from simple changes in the weather to traumatizing world news, looming deadlines, pollution, a cold, blood pressure changes, hunger, feelings of fatigue, inflammation, sleep deprivation, eating processed foods, or emotional stress. Stress can manifest as real, life-threatening challenges or hidden stressors like the act of worrying, feelings of low self-worth, or a faulty immune system that can't mount a strong antibody response.

To the brain, anything that challenges the body's homeostasis qualifies as stress, and it doesn't matter whether it is physical, psychological, emotional, real, or imagined. As long as the brain perceives that your state of balance is being challenged, it counts as stress, and with that, a physiological stress response is always mounted so that the problem can be solved and you can adapt and ultimately survive.

The Stress Response

The stress response, or the physiological response to stress, exists for good reason. It gets you out of bed in the morning, gets your immune system to fight infections, your blood vessels to maintain your blood pressure, your body to move when you are uncomfortable, and your sensory system to tell you when you are hungry, cold, or tired. Without the stress response, you essentially would be dead because it enables wounds to be healed, traumas to be survived, nutritional needs to be met, and escape to take place when you are being chased by a lion.

Walter Cannon, a Harvard physiologist, coined the term "fight or flight" in the 1930s to describe our inborn defense response to threat or danger. He believed this defense is meant to ultimately ensure survival.[1] When we face a threat or danger, we are catapulted to move because of the release of stress hormones like adrenalin and cortisol into the bloodstream, which causes our senses to become hyperalert and aroused, our pupils to dilate, and our muscles to tense up in preparation for battle or flight. The liver releases stored sugar into the bloodstream to provide your body with energy, while the lungs work faster, increasing your breathing rate and causing the breath to be more shallow to economize on oxygen consumption. The heart pumps harder and faster, blood pressure rises, and the immune system is provoked to mount an inflammatory response to protect you from being slowed down by a possible wound or infection.

This physiological response is great when you are being chased by a saber-tooth tiger or a mugger, and in the short term in most cases, it creates physical, emotional, or psychological discomfort of one kind or another that serve to motivate you into action. For instance, if your blood sugar drops, the stress response will be triggered to initiate a series of physiological changes that will cause you to feel hungry, irritable, or tired. This discomfort or negative feeling then motivates you to eat something to make the hunger or bad feeling go away so that you can get back into balance or comfort again. Eating then results in the stress being extinguished so that the stress response is no longer needed. The stress response will shut itself off, allowing your system to resume its state of balance.

This is the good news when it comes to stress and the stress response.

The bad news is that your brain can't tell the difference between one stress and another. It can't distinguish between running for your life and running late to work because both are deemed threats to your livelihood somewhere in the recesses of your brain. For this reason, the stress response is set off too often, and much of the time, it doesn't get shut off because the stress never gets taken care of, like a persistent worry.

In the 1950s, Hans Selye expanded on Cannon's work and explained that you do not have to be chased by a raging animal for the fight or flight response to be mounted; this heightened reaction occurs regardless of whether the challenge at hand is life-threatening or not.[2] You could be late for work, be worried about paying your bills, think you are going to get fired, or think that your spouse is going to leave you. The physiological response is the same:

- Pupils dilate
- Blood vessels constrict in hands and feet and gut
- Gastrointestinal tract shuts down; slower movement of the colon, etc.
- Reproductive system shuts down
- Muscles become tense, especially back, neck, jaw, shoulders, etc.
- Immune system causes more inflammation, clotting, and allergic reactions (over time, poor immunity against infections or cancers)
- Cardiovascular system increases in heart rate and blood pressure
- Respiratory system increases in breathing rate and inflammation
- Brain engages in less complex thinking, hyper-alertness, and arousal; more fear-related behaviors initiated
- Mood takes a dive as loss of serotonin and other neurotransmitters cause depression, anxiety, fear, anger, and other negative emotions

Normally, the body has a built-in mechanism to turn the stress response off once a stress or challenge has been taken care of, so that as long as the stress response is short-lived, the physiological changes are beneficial to the body. But when the threat is ongoing—like a constant worry, a deep feeling of being unworthy, an abusive family member, or chronic pollution exposure—the stress response does not shut down. Not only does an over-active stress response then lead to a host of physical problems, but it also leads to a constant negative state of mind, perception, belief, and mood.

Stress, or the perception of stress, has everything to do with your bad mood, negative emotions, or inability to control your anger.

Perception Is Key

You might be thinking to yourself right now that you are doomed because you are always stressed, meaning your stress response is always active, which is also why you are always angry or sick. Don't despair. You have the ability to fix the problem by learning how to change your perception of yourself and your life.

The key to keeping the stress response under control is perception. If your brain perceived a particular situation to be manageable, it would fire the stress response only long enough to motivate the necessary action, like an athlete who is motivated to compete and win a race. It's basically what you would call having a positive outlook. Positive perception is directly correlated to inner surety or trust in success or manageability of a particular endeavor or challenge. Negative perception, in contrast, is associated with lower self-appraisal and belief in the possibility of a positive outcome occurring.

For example, you may agonize over a choice of school for your child. You agonize night and day over this issue until it feels like your life is spinning out of control. Your anxiety triggers the stress response, which causes your heart rate and blood pressure to rise, inflammation to course through your body, your memory to feel hazy, and your cravings for comfort food or alcohol to skyrocket. You feel tired and achy and overwhelmed by the demands of your life. You simply don't think you can handle much more. Then your child, spouse, boss, or fill-in-the-blank person acts rudely or out of order and your temper then gets the best of you and everyone else. The shame you experience from your behavior makes you feel even worse, exacerbating the stress response further, and the cycle rages on.

Now if you were able to change your mindset to believe that whatever choice you made would be okay, the scenario would play out very differently.

For instance, you feel very confident about your ability to make choices and are also confident there is no such thing as a wrong choice because every choice brings opportunity for growth and learning. You know that no matter what school you send your child to, the school will be perfect, or you will find ways to make it work. You have a similar attitude to most of the demands in your life, knowing how to delegate and find help when you need to. In this case, do you think you would blow up when said child, spouse, boss, or fill-in-the-blank person acts rudely? Probably not. Why?

Perception.

When you perceive stress to be manageable, you gain control over the stress response and over your reactions. Perception is actually the key to being resilient. The more you believe in your own ability and resources to handle adversity, the more likely you are to perceive stress as manageable, leading to less worry, more confidence, a stronger sense of self-value, positive expectation, a controlled stress response, and a stronger you.

If you were to operate from a *positive* perception that resources will be available to handle any uncertainty, you would step forward in life with more surety, knowing you could deal with whatever came your way. You would be able to maintain a sense of calm, even when someone is acting rudely or disrespectfully. Your stress levels would remain controlled; physical health, stable; and mental and emotional clarity, intact.

Awareness Leads to Better Perception

If it were easy to maintain a positive perception and keep the stress response under control, I wouldn't be writing this book for you—or have a job, for that matter. The catch is that you need to be aware you are stressed and take care of it before it gets control of you. You may not be aware, for instance, that the sleep deprivation you are experiencing as a result of your pushing yourself to succeed at work is inducing inflammation in your body and creating more stress. You may also not be aware that you are holding onto memories that no longer serve you. These memories still define you and your perception and drive you to succeed at your body's expense. You may not realize that at your core you believe you are not good enough and you have been living in constant stress your whole life.

Awareness of Emotions and Memories

Emotions and emotional memory are directly connected to physiological responses, both positive and negative. Any time you experience a particular emotion, your brain will search its emotional memory bank to bring forward assumptions, beliefs, behaviors, and physiological and physical reactions that helped you cope in the past. When faced with challenges that elicit an emotion in you, the brain searches its memory bank for details to see how such challenges have been handled previously, what resources were used, and what the outcome may have been and match the information with your emotional memory bank. The outcome is a reaction and behavior to said challenge that is motivated by a now unconscious belief and assumption.

Over the course of your lifetime, as one memory builds up upon the other, a belief system forms regarding how you see yourself, others, and the world around you, either positive—that you are enough and have enough—or negative—that you are not enough or don't have enough. Most people hold different beliefs depending on the situation. For instance, the same person can believe that there will always be enough money because he or she grew up wealthy, but there is never enough love, as there was no love afforded in the home. Some of your beliefs, therefore, uphold positive expectations that your future needs will be met. Other beliefs, based on more hurtful experiences, have taken on a more negative stance, upholding negative expectations that you may never be or have enough, and that the world or people can't be trusted to help you. The result is that situations arising today can trigger a positive or negative physiological response and subsequent belief and behavior, based on the memory.

For example, if in your past your family always had enough money and all your needs were always met, you will likely believe today that you will always have enough of whatever you need. In contrast, if you grew up having food on the table and clothes on your body but your parents constantly worried about money, you will likely share some of this worry too. As an adult now, even though you have a stable income, you still may question, "What if I won't be provided for? What if I don't have enough money?" You worry daily and stay at a job you don't like even though you dream of doing something else, and you essentially feel trapped. (Can you see how this may be a setup for resentment, frustration, and easily blowing up?)

Another example might be that your boss, colleague, or friend is disrespecting you or not taking your advice. If in your past you were often criticized and put down, this type of situation may trigger you to get extremely upset and angry, more so than someone else might who was rarely criticized. Every time you are criticized, this memory gets triggered. When you are triggered, you do what you have always done to cope—you scream, eat, withdraw, and so forth. Though the behavior helps you cope short term, it solves nothing and in the end usually makes you feel worse.

The following self-awareness exercise will help you see how emotions can lead to a different mindset and how memories can play a role in how your mind and body react.

Exercise 1.1: Self-Awareness

1. Think about a situation that made you angry, resentful, or frustrated.
2. Now pay attention to how it makes you feel. Become aware of the sensations you are experiencing in your body, particularly your chest, jaw, and stomach, as well as the movement of your breath. Where is the emotion lodging in your body? What does it feel like? Does the body feel tense, constricted, restricted?
3. Notice how strong the emotion is and if it escalates the more you think about the situation. Notice the thoughts themselves and write them down if you like. What are you really angry about?
4. Contemplate if these thoughts and feelings align with feelings of being enough or not enough and why.

If a large part of your belief system is a fear that you will never or may never be enough or have enough, the stress response will be active constantly. You will be easily triggered to feel angry, fearful, or upset, especially when facing challenges that remind you of a hurtful memory.

When triggers, negative emotions, and underlying negative beliefs are addressed, you have a better chance of regulating the stress response, controlling anger and other negative emotions, and being able to maintain an enhanced peace of mind and a healthier body.

Awareness of Beliefs

Always remember that you are not your memories and whatever happened to you in the past does not determine your value. The problem is that when you were a child, you did not possess much of a brain yet. In other words, when bad things happened to you, your brain interpreted the situation based on limited knowledge and skills. A belief created from that vantage point was often distorted and untrue. It is this illogical and untrue belief that drives your stress response and negative behaviors.

If you were to consciously focus on changing the belief so that eventually a new one took a form that is more positive, logical, and true, you would have a much better handle on your reactions and stress. There are many techniques available in the psychological and spiritual healing worlds, including cognitive restructuring strategies and a variety of meditation practices, that I will discuss in this book. The point is that you have the ability to influence any change in a positive or a negative direction by the choices you make that are based on beliefs that you hold.

It is possible to disassociate negative emotions and beliefs from unhappy memories and reprogram the brain with positive emotions and expectations of trust. You can learn to perceive situations differently so that they appear more manageable to you. More importantly, you can learn to see yourself differently, knowing that you are truly valuable, loved, and supported. When you do so, very little can shake you.

In the following self-awareness exercise, you can observe the difference an emotion can make on your peception.

Exercise 1.2: Self-Awareness

1. Think about a situation that made you angry, resentful, or frustrated.
2. Now pay attention to how it makes you feel. Become aware of the sensations you are experiencing in your body, particularly your chest, jaw, and stomach, as well as the movement of your breath. Where is the emotion lodging in your body? What does it feel like? Does the body feel tense, constricted, restricted?
3. Notice how strong the emotion is and if it escalates the more you think about the situation. Notice the thoughts themselves and write them down if you like. What are you really angry about?
4. Contemplate if these thoughts and feelings align with feelings of being enough or not enough and why.
5. Now redirect your focus and think about a situation of awe, love, or laughter. For instance, remember how it felt to be looked at by someone who absolutely adores you, watching your child walk for the first time, gazing at an incredible sunset, or laughing so hard you couldn't breathe.
6. Continue to focus on this memory and feeling, and notice how your body feels.
7. Now go back to thinking about the situation of anger and notice if you feel or think differently.

You might have observed in this exercise the difference in how you feel when angry versus happy or disrespected versus loved. Hopefully, after connecting with a happier memory, you felt less charged when you thought about the stressful situation again. By changing your emotion and the associated physiological state from negative to positive, you changed the vantage point from which you were viewing the situation, invariably changing your perception to one of more positive expectation.

Getting in Control

I have found that when my patients choose to see themselves as having enough and being enough, they become healthier, more resilient, and calmer in the face of adversity. In contrast, the patients who consider themselves victims of life's circumstances are less likely to handle challenges effectively and are more likely to succumb to negative emotional, psychological, and physical complaints.

Always remember that you have the ability to influence your life in a positive or a negative direction by the choices you make and the perception you hold, especially with regard to the stress in your life and how you see yourself within the larger world. When you uphold a positive mindset or perception, you keep the stress response in check and you function from a place of feeling whole and content versus empty and pissed off. You feel in control.

Your ability to maintain a positive mindset and perception depends on three factors:

1. Your past experiences, memories, and beliefs, especially with regard to how they made you feel about yourself and your resources. As I explained in brief previously, these will influence your perception, especially when you are in a negative mood or state of mind.

2. Your mood, whether positive or negative. You hopefully noticed the difference your mood and emotional state had on the outcome of the self-awareness exercise.

3. Your supportive infrastructure, which allows you to maintain an open mind and resilient body and get to the belief that you have what it takes to find and be in your bliss. This infrastructure includes how much sleep you get, how well you take care of yourself (exercise, nutrition, meditation, etc.), how strong your social support system is, how often you play and laugh, how connected you are to spiritual practices and beliefs, and how often you spend time in nature.

Over the course of this book, I will give you the tools and techniques that will help you heal your beliefs, keep a positive mood and mindset, and build your infrastructure. You will learn to quiet your mind and calm your body to turn down the stress response, while also learning to have compassion for and not judge whatever you feel in recognition that you are being triggered. You will learn to be mindful of your emotions, thoughts, and body's physiological reactions, be guided by them rather than react because of them, and eventually detach from your anger. Ultimately, you will learn how to access feelings of joy, love, and compassion; to find your power; and to not give a damn because you have found your bliss.

Chapter 2
Get a Hold on Negative Emotions

....

"If you try to get rid of fear and anger without knowing their meaning, they will grow stronger and return."

—Deepak Chopra, *The Third Jesus: The Christ We Cannot Ignore*

Negative emotions are meant to alert you that something is amiss, drive you to get away from danger, stand up for yourself and for those you love, or take the time to grieve so that you can heal and move forward. Negative emotions push you to take action and force change when change is due through the stimulation of the stress response. Out of all the negative emotions or states—fear, anger, grief, anxiety, and depression—anger is the one emotion that most people repress or express when under stress—whether as a result of frustration, indignation, stagnation, or feeling overwhelmed—and then feel bad about it or themselves, which creates more stress and distress. Out of all the negative emotions, anger is also the most powerful. It can cause massive destruction when uncontrolled or incredible change for the good when used correctly.

In the Five Element System of traditional Chinese medicine, every negative emotion is associated with different internal organs, seasons, energies, and even foods or cravings. The energy of anger is seen to be explosive, so powerful that it can move mountains and mold landscapes like a strong wind.[3] When the energy of anger is transformed for good, it can motivate positive change and correction of injustice. When the energy is left to do its bidding, like an explosion or a hurricane, it can rage out of control, leaving chaos and destruction in its wake.

The key is to be able to transmute this powerful energy force so that you use it to become more empowered, to benefit yourself and others, rather than to demolish and destroy. The first step in this process involves acknowledging and allowing yourself to feel.

Validating and Understanding the Self

Do you allow yourself to feel, and especially to be angry?

Many of us have been taught to believe that stress is bad and that to be angry is even worse. We either squash our feelings or feel guilty if we yell or act rudely or negatively. The problem is that when you repress your feelings, the stress simply implodes internally. Like a soda can that is shaken when closed, you eventually combust. Ignoring your feelings or putting them down only causes wounds to deepen, not heal.

Exercise 2.1: Attuning to Feelings

A. Fill in the blank of the following statement using as many words as seem applicable. Do not think about each word. Only spend enough time to contemplate being angry or stressed and then choose the words that come to mind.

"When I act out in anger, I feel _____."

Word choices:

Acceptable	Aggressive	Alienated	Amazed	Anxious
Ashamed	Astonished	Awed	Awful	Confident
Confused	Courageous	Critical	Despair	Detestable
Devastated	Disappointed	Embarrassed	Empty	Energized
Frightened	Fulfilled	Guilty	Hateful	Hopeful
Hostile	Humiliated	Hurt	Important	Inadequate
Indifferent	Infuriated	Insignificant	Inspired	Isolated
Joyful	Liberated	Loathing	Lonely	Optimistic

Overwhelmed	Peaceful	Powerful	Powerless	Proud
Rejected	Relieved	Remorseful	Respected	Satisfied
Scared	Shocked	Terrified	Victimized	Vulnerable
Withdrawn	Wonderful	Worried	Worthless	Worthy

B. Now separate the words into two columns, positive and negative, and notice how many words land in each column.

Many of you will find that you associated getting stressed or angry with a lot of negativity. You might also find that you wrote down some positive feelings as well, like feeling powerful, satisfied, or liberated. Indeed, expressing anger or pent-up feelings from stress can be a powerful experience of release, like a pressure cooker finally letting out all of its steam, and you may have noted that in your choice of words.

Have you ever dug deep enough to understand where your anger or stress is coming from? I am not just referring to your stress that is a result of a horrible boss or a spouse who doesn't listen to you. I am referring to the negative feelings that come with feeling mistreated or neglected, like humiliated or disrespected. Have you ever really looked at the true source of your feelings that is leading you to react or be triggered in the first place, bad situation or not?

The true source reflects how you perceive yourself within your world—victim or victor. Noting down the different words that describe how you might feel pinpoint this perception. If you feel disrespected, for instance, you may want to ask yourself if feeling disrespected is a pattern for you. Or if you feel empowered when you express anger, you may want to delve deeper into why you need a powerful yet destructive emotion to enable you to feel empowered.

The point of this exercise is for you to become aware of your own attitudes and feelings related to being stressed and angry, both positive and negative, so that you can dig deeper into your own beliefs and perceptions.

For instance, you find yourself upset with your spouse because he or she did not support your authority when it came to punishing your kids. If you were to label the underlying feeling, you may note you are feeling infuriated, disrespected, or victimized. You then might delve deeper by asking yourself why you are feeling infuriated, disrespected, or victimized, and you discover that the situation is causing you to feel unsupported and alone. When you think further about this state of being, you realize that feeling unsupported and alone has been a common theme for you for a long time, perhaps your whole life. You also realize that when you feel unsupported and alone, you tend to react in a similar fashion each time. In other words, you notice a pattern.

Creating such categories as "feeling unsupported" invariably will help you validate and label your feelings, help you understand yourself better, and allow you to objectify any situation and your emotions more easily in the future, which gives you the opportunity to apply antidotes or remedies that help you get more balanced.

Creating your categories involves a four-step process:

1. Validate and note down your feelings, acknowledging to yourself that a valid reason exists that is causing your distress.
2. Witness your physiology by taking note of your physical and emotional reactions—what you feel in your body, where you feel the tension, and what emotions are rising up for you.
3. Observe the reason for your distress, uncovering why you feel the way you do.
4. Notice how you express or react.

This four-step process allows you to make a connection between the reasons you get distressed, how your body reacts, what your underlying beliefs and perceptions are, and how you ultimately react or express yourself when distressed—which may be particular to you.

The following exercise will guide you on how to create a category by observing your feelings, emotions, physical sensations, and reactions and the way you express yourself or behave given a stressful situation.

Exercise 2.2: Creating a Category

You are rushing to get to a meeting or an appointment and have just enough time to stop for a coffee at a nearby café. You open the door to the café, only to be shoved out of the way by a man who gets in line ahead of you and orders five complicated lattes.

A. Write down how you feel, using the words from the chart.

_____

_____

_____

_____

B. Take a moment to observe the physical reaction that occurs in your body when you imagine this scenario happening to you, along with the emotions that rise up. Does your chest tighten? Does your stomach contract? Do you hold your breath or start breathing more shallowly? Write down the physical reaction that you experience.

_____

_____

_____

_____

C. How do you react? Would you speak up and say something to this person? Would you clam up and clench your teeth, keeping it all in? Would you storm off without your coffee and slam the door? Would you keep quiet but snap at your daughter when she calls you on the phone at the office? Would you soothe yourself by ordering two donuts because you deserve it for what you've been through? Write down how you might normally behave.

_____

_____

_____

_____

_____

_____

_____

_____

_____

Causes for Distress

At its basic level, stress or distress usually arises because you perceive you or those you love are being threatened.

Now remember that your brain doesn't distinguish between real or imagined threats, big or small. That threat, in other words, could come in the form of disrespect, humiliation, fear of criticism, or loss. Whatever the threat, it will elicit the stress response and an automated reaction and behavior, meaning that it will lead to a physical reaction and a behavior or action to follow.

There are many situations, therefore, that will give rise to distress, from the mundane to the serious. In the following exercise, I list some of the causes or situations that lead to distress. Take note of your own reactions, patterns, and behaviors. Answer the questions and then fill in the blanks.

Exercise 2.3: Examining Categories

A. Feeling unsupported

Many situations can lead you to feeling unsupported, including a spouse who doesn't back you up when you try to discipline your children, a friend who doesn't support your point of view, colleagues who undermine you in front of your superiors, a job that doesn't pay you enough, or a lack of money in your bank account. Feeling unsupported usually leads to feeling overburdened, resentful, fatigued, overwhelmed, and unhappy as you work harder to be validated, pay your bills, or keep your family together without much help.

- Do I often get upset because I feel unsupported? Y/N
- Am I always the one helping others and doing all the giving and not being helped? Y/N
- Am I the one listening and understanding others but not being understood myself? Y/N
- Do I often feel overwhelmed? Y/N

- Do I feel that my needs are being met? Y/N
- When I feel unsupported, I _____.

B. Being ignored and invisible

I don't know anyone who likes being ignored, and at a core level, feeling invisible is akin to feeling that one's existence is not valuable or valued. Perhaps you seem to always be passed over for a promotion, or you often find yourself talking to your spouse or friend and realize that he or she is not listening. Maybe you find that when you are with a group of people, you are ignored and no one pays attention to your contributions. You feel as if you don't exist. How do you react when you are ignored?

- Do I often feel invisible? Y/N
- Do my children, spouse, partner, friends often ignore me? Y/N
- Have I got passed over for promotions, leads, or jobs in favor of someone else who is more visible? Y/N
- Am I often made to feel like I don't exist? Y/N
- When I feel ignored, I _____.

C. Rejection

Being ignored may also feel like rejection. Rejection involves feeling shunned or pushed away by another person or entity. When someone you hold dear or with high regard rejects you, the pain can often be overwhelming, as happens when a relationship ends, you get fired, or you don't get a job you applied for. Feeling rejected can bring up deeper feelings of not being worthy, loved, valued, or wanted. Some people are more rejection sensitive than others, which is very much influenced by early life experiences involving love and acceptance by one's family, peers, or teachers. The more you experience rejection, the more likely you are also to reject yourself. You may also interpret the downs that come along with the ups of life as rejection.

- Am I more prone to getting angry or depressed when rejected? Y/N
- Do I tend to shut down and stop interacting or paying attention to the people I am with when rejected? Y/N
- When life isn't going well, do I tend to feel like I am being punished? Y/N
- Do I tend to avoid situations like dating or trying a new job for fear I may be rejected? Y/N
- When I feel rejected, I _____.

D. Humiliation

When humiliated, you perceive that your social status has been diminished and your pride or dignity lost. You may feel like dirt, foolish, ashamed, powerless, or helpless. Humiliating experiences can be extremely traumatic and may cut deep into your psyche and sense of Self, especially when they occur earlier in life when your brain is forming and you are figuring out who you are.

- Do I get upset or argumentative when told I am wrong? Y/N
- If someone were to pull me aside to correct my behavior, would I feel insulted or embarrassed? Y/N
- If someone were to put me down, would I feel like I needed to get retaliation or revenge? Y/N
- Do I have a tendency to assume others are looking down on me so that I become easily slighted? Y/N
- Do I often feel unappreciated? Y/N
- When I feel humiliated, I _____.

E. Injustice

At some point, everyone faces situations that are unfair. But does an unfair situation always warrant anxiety or rage? The extent to which you react to feelings of injustice or unfairness is ultimately based on how personally you take the situation. Injustice can come in the form of having a thief violate your property, being wrongly accused, being discriminated against, or the feeling that the universe is throwing you hard luck and no one else, or that a lover has betrayed you.

- Do I often feel that situations are unfair? Y/N
- Do I have a tendency to feel the need to fight for justice politically but also find this translates to fighting with others in my life? Y/N
- When I think about someone who has betrayed me, is the first thing I want to do is get revenge? Y/N
- Could I easily make a list of the unfair things in my life? Y/N
- When I feel an injustice has been done to me, I _____.

F. Let down or disappointment

Let's say you have a friend that more often than not cancels at the last minute. If this were to happen once, you might feel disappointed. But if this were to be a regular occurrence, your disappointment might turn into anger and resentment, or even depression. The extent to which you get angry is dependent on your expectations. If you expected your friend to cancel and had made alternative plans just in case, would you be as angry? If a waiter ignores you, a doctor makes you wait an hour, or a friend makes other plans without you, do you shrug it off, or do you get upset? Look closely at your own expectations of yourself and others.

- If I were to think about the last time or the last person that caused me disappointment, would I still feel emotionally charged about it or upset? Y/N
- Do I often get upset with others for not meeting my expectations? Y/N
- Do I get upset with myself for not meeting my own expectations? Y/N
- Do I recall being frequently disappointed in my childhood? Y/N
- When I feel disappointed, I _____.

G. Grief or loss

Losing someone or something you love can leave you feeling broken and incomplete and full of regret, guilt, or remorse. Sadness, anger, denial, and depression often accompany the experience of loss. Loss can result in feelings of helplessness to change an unjust situation, abandonment by someone you hold dear, regret or guilt because you could have done something differently, or shaming or blaming yourself for someone's absence.

- Am I still grieving the loss of someone I held dear? Y/N
- Do I blame myself for what happened or believe that I could have done something differently or better that I didn't do? Y/N
- Am I angry with this person for leaving me? Y/N
- Am I angry with an establishment or other person for not doing more to save this person? Y/N
- When I feel grief, I _____.

H. Illness or physical complaints

When you are not feeling well, aren't you more easily irritated? Physical issues normally heighten the stress response, giving you less wiggle room when it comes to maintaining your emotional and mental balance. Even simple sleep deprivation can lead to the smallest situation setting off a heightened stress response. In addition to being more on edge—if you are like some of my patients—you may be angry with your body for betraying you, angry that you are sick in the first place, aggrieved that you can't do the things you used to do, enraged at the unfairness of being dealt such a bad deck of cards, or you may hold a keener sense of rejection that you are not like normal people and therefore feel you are undesirable. When one suffers from an illness, any or all of the reasons or causes for distress can apply.

- Do I feel "less than" because I have physical or psychological problems? Y/N
- Am I angry with my body for not doing what I want it to do? Y/N
- Am I easily overwhelmed because I get so tired? Y/N
- If I am hungry or sleep deprived, am I more irritable? Y/N
- When I feel sick, I _____.

Did any of these examples hit a nerve for you? Most of us have one or two buttons, that, when pressed, catapult us into a heightened stress reaction. For now, take note of which of the scenarios most applied to you or elicited the more prominent or charged response.

How We Express Distress

Essentially, there are three major ways distress is expressed: externally, internally, or peacefully. You either 1) scream and blow up, 2) swallow your feelings and internally combust, or 3) use reason, breath, love, or humor to work through the hurt, find reason and compassion, and eventually manage a situation peacefully. The goal, of course, is for you to do the latter as often as possible, because both externally and internally expressing your distress can lead to negative health and life consequences. In contrast, the better you are at soothing stress, healing underlying beliefs and hurts, and communicating your thoughts and feelings peacefully, the healthier you will be.

The next exercise will offer examples of both external and internal expressers. The exercise following will give you a case scenario so that you can assess more clearly what sort of expresser you may be. Answer the questions thoughtfully.

Exercise 2.4: Assessing Your Reaction and Behaviors

Read the following scenario, then choose the response that most represents your reaction.

You have made plans with your significant other to see a movie. You have wanted to see this particular movie for months and have been planning this outing for a long time. Your significant other sends you a message that he or she can't make it due to working late, leaving you feeling disappointed, though you try to understand. A few days later, you are on the phone with a mutual friend, Eve, who tells you she saw your significant other at a new restaurant and asked if the person he or she was with was a work colleague. You then find out that this took place on the same evening the two of you were meant to go see a movie. You realize you have been lied to and blown off.

How do you react?

A. Feeling hurt, humiliated, and betrayed, as soon as you get off the phone with Eve, you call your significant other and ream him or her out, accusing them of lying and cheating. Profanities leave your mouth in succession. You throw his or her clothes out the window and rip up all the photos of the two of you. You drive to a bar, drink your sorrows away, drive home drunk, and pass out. You wake up the next morning feeling like you got run over by a Mack truck, emotionally and physically. You decide to stay drunk for the rest of the week and leave threatening voice mails on your significant other's phone.

B. You do not say anything to Eve or call your significant other. Instead, you load yourself up with ice cream and any other junk food you can find, stuffing down your feelings as much as possible. You decide to pretend that you never heard anything, that it didn't happen, and you look the other way. When you see your significant other, you act as if nothing is wrong, though you stop offering sex or cooking dinner. He/she asks you if there is anything wrong, and you repeatedly say, "Everything is fine."

C. When you get off the phone, you continue to ruminate and bounce back and forth between being angry and hurt, trying to find a rational explanation for your significant other's behavior and plotting a way to avenge yourself. Rather than confront him/her that evening or the next day, you avoid his/her calls for a week or more, waiting until you are ready to face him/her. The whole time, as you continue to vacillate between despair and revenge, you stalk his/her Facebook page.

D. As soon as you get off the phone, you take a few moments to connect with what you are feeling. You recognize that you are feeling betrayed, lied to, humiliated, and hurt. You understand that no matter what the excuse, your significant partner lied to you and that is never okay. You acknowledge that you have every right to be angry and upset, take deep breaths, fill your heart with love, and decide you need to do some self-nurturing because you can't think straight. You take a bath and write in your journal. Though you still find yourself feeling upset and hurt, you also acknowledge that you value yourself, your time, and your integrity. The next day you ask your partner to meet you for coffee and tell him/her how you feel and that you cannot tolerate lying, that the trust is broken, and that the relationship will need to end, at least for now. You listen to the explanation, but you hold steady on your decision to take care of yourself.

Evaluating your response

Answer A is clearly an example of expressing distress externally, both at the other person and at yourself through the act of self-abuse via alcohol overconsumption. Answer B represents a person who is expressing distress internally, while answer C reflects a combination of the two. The last case exemplifies a peaceful warrior who first takes their own feelings into account, honors the way he/she feels, and takes care of themselves with love and respect so that communication and resolution are more possible.

To look further into what sort of expresser you might be, do the next exercise.

Exercise 2.5: Assessing External Versus Internal Expressions of Distress

A. The external expresser

External expressers can't be missed, tending to openly scream, yell, hit, bully, or threaten, cry, or be general drama queens or kings. Flying into a rage or becoming melodramatic, even with small problems, and using illogical arguments while attacking others verbally or otherwise qualifies as external expressions of distress. To see if you may be one to express distress externally, answer the following questions:

Do you . . .

- Bully other people to do what you want by using your physical, financial, or authoritative power over their weakness? Y/N
- Use name-calling, objectifying, and swearing or physical abuse of any kind when arguing? Y/N
- Destroy property that belongs to the subject of your distress, your own belongings, or random property that happens to be in your way? Y/N
- Abandon others by refusing to communicate, answer calls, or go to work (i.e., quit your job)? Y/N
- Threaten to hurt others or yourself, or act in a threatening manner? Y/N
- Feel justified in getting revenge on those you believe have hurt you? Y/N
- Blame or accuse others openly for negative outcomes without taking responsibility for your own actions? Y/N
- Act selfishly in your belief that you are a victim and act entitled by cutting people off in traffic, ignoring other people's needs, or doing whatever you want despite the effects your actions may have on others? Y/N
- Openly cry or complain, letting the world know of your problems and victimized state? Y/N

B. The internal expresser

People who internally express distress often appear to be calm at all times as their distress is well-hidden, muted, or repressed. If you are an internal expresser then, even though you do not yell, scream, or cry in public, you internalize your feelings, sometimes so deeply that you might not even realize you are in distress. This is very common when it comes to anger, as many people tend to repress this emotion. To see if you may be an internal expresser, answer the following questions:

Do you . . .

- Avoid confrontation, conflict, or issues that need talking about? Y/N
- Avoid communication, look the other way, or bury your head in the ground, hoping a problem will go away on its own? Y/N
- Procrastinate, hoping an issue will resolve itself over time so that you don't have to take action? Y/N
- Manipulate or try to influence people or situations to do or be what you need them to, avoiding upset? Y/N
- Withdraw into yourself when upset, becoming sullen and sulky with self-pity, which also draws sympathy from others? Y/N
- Avoid showing up on time or at all, withhold love or stop doing things you normally do for or with others (like sex, cook, clean, drive, and so forth) as a passive-aggressive way of controlling someone or a situation without blatantly saying anything? Y/N
- Blame others for your misfortunes, acting as a misfortunate and as a victim without taking responsibility for your own role? Y/N
- Blame yourself instead of others by withholding care, love, or nurture, invariably inflicting anger or injury on yourself? Y/N
- Over-rationalize and intellectualize a situation to avoid being angry or expressing emotions without fully connecting to your feelings? Y/N

Learning from Your Reactions to Become a Peaceful Warrior

There is nothing wrong with being an external or internal expresser, other than it usually makes you and/or other people more miserable. The key is to learn about yourself, your own reactions and patterns, so that you can eventually heal yourself and change underlying beliefs from negative to positive so that you no longer get triggered. If you are not triggered, the stress response does not get out of control. When the stress response is in control, so are you, enabling you to be calmer, connect with reason, and express yourself clearly and strongly, like a peaceful warrior.

Being a peaceful warrior does not mean not taking action, and I have used the term "warrior" to make sure of that. If injustice has been done, it is usually necessary to do something. But you want the something to be constructive and helpful, not destructive.

As you move forward, you will be learning how to be more mindful of your body and it's reactions, your emotions and how they influence you to react. You will also be developing new ways to heal and become more powerful and, ultimately, blissful. Along the way, you will fill out a Distress Assessment Chart, which will help you to see the connections between your feelings, reactions, and responses. You can begin to fill out the chart now by writing in your answers and observations from the previous exercises.

Distress Assessment Chart

What happened?	What is my physical reaction?	How is it making me feel?	How do I react?	What can I do to heal?	What is my new response?
Unsupported					
Ignored					
Rejection					
Humiliation					
Injustice					
Disappointment					

Grief/loss				
Illness/pain				

The following is an example of how to fill out a Distress Assessment Chart. For now, though, simply fill out the first four columns. The rest you will learn how to do as we go forward. Onward!

Sample Distress Assessment Chart

What happened?	What is my physical reaction?	How is it making me feel?	How do I react?	What can I do to heal?	What is my new response?
Rejection	Ache in heart area	Unwanted	Shut down; withdraw	Heal the heart with self-acceptance	Don't care; know there is something better
Unsupported	Tension in back	Alone	Irritable; easily lash out on others	Improve the infrastructure	Stronger and aware of my needs
Injustice	Tension in upper back and chest	Disrespected; hurt	Shut down and lash out on strangers	Meditate and connect with something pure (nature, spirituality, etc.)	Compassion for myself and those who feel necessary to lie and hurt

Chapter 3
Zap Distress with Love

....

"Where there is anger there is always pain underneath."
—Eckhart Tolle, *The Power of Now*

Without suffering or pain, there exists little reason for rage. If you think about a four-year-old girl who is hurt, how does she react? Does she cry out or have a tantrum, or does she talk her way out of whatever she is feeling, find reason, and use her words wisely to express herself?

When you are triggered and distressed, you become like this four-year-old child, where reason, rationale, and compassion get thrown out the window because the stress response sends signals to higher brain centers like the prefrontal cortex to shut down, while signaling lower, more primitive brain centers such as the amygdala to take over. As the amygdala is activated, negative emotions escalate as hurtful and negative memories are brought forward, signaling the stress response to fire more strongly. Tunnel vision takes over and eventually what may have started out as a bit of stress transforms into raging distress. Trying to stop this process once it starts is akin to trying to stop a shiver when you are freezing cold, which is close to impossible. However, there do exist experienced meditators and monks who are capable of regulating their own body temperature through breath work and meditation.

My point is that it is possible to get control over the stress response, shift out of this negative state, and access your higher mind, rationale, and sense of calm. It may take a little work to get there, but it's possible, especially if you learn to heal old wounds with a lot of love.

The Memories That Trigger Distress

Though it is rare that your life is actually being threatened, your brain does not usually distinguish between real or imagined threats. If a threat is perceived to be severe, the amygdala is activated to take over, and fear and fear-related behaviors take precedence over your rational brain and thinking abilities. If the threat is perceived to be mild, the amygdala will work alongside higher brain centers, which influence the amygdala to fire less strongly, thus provoking a weaker stress response with less associated negative emotions, which allows for better access to calm and rational thinking and behaviors. In other words, when you perceive that a threat is mild and not life-threatening, you are better able to motivate sound action without losing your cool.

The problem lies in the fact that much of the time you are not aware that you perceive a given stress as life-threatening or severe because it is your unconscious mind (not conscious) via your memory bank that is feeling threatened. In such a case, your brain will remember an old memory of being hurt, and a threat that is minor in reality is perceived by the brain as severe. The prefrontal cortex and other higher brain centers shut down, causing the stress response to charge faster and stronger, despite your knowing better.

Most of your memories, especially the ones that are associated with strong emotions, aren't necessarily accurate but are associated with assumptions and beliefs that you developed during the course of your life. Different situations can bring these memories forward as well as the associated assumptions, beliefs, and behaviors. A stressful situation might trigger a painful memory, which propels negative assumptions and beliefs that eventually lead to a pattern of behavior. The behavior may be explosive in nature, one of avoidance, passive aggressiveness, abusive (to Self or others), and so forth. The deeper or more hurtful the memory, the easier it is to trigger the automatic response.

Painful memories can also be brought forward when a situation is barely even stressful because you are not taking care of yourself or you feel vulnerable or physical ill. This can happen when you are sleep-deprived, full of toxic chemicals (from food or alcohol) that create negative physiology in your body, in financial distress, overwhelmed with life's responsibilities, having difficulties in a relationship or work, or experiencing any other sort of stress that leads you feeling more victim than victor.

The point here is that as long as you are feeling victimized, or you consciously or unconsciously uphold a belief that you are victimized, distress will play a major role in your life. And believe it or not, one way to correct this problem is by having compassion for yourself.

A Little Compassion Goes a Long Way

Imagine you have a four-year-old daughter. She has come to you angry and is having a tantrum at the playground. What do you do?

- Yell at your daughter for making a scene and punish her with a timeout.
- Try to comfort her and then see if you can find a solution.
- Does your reaction depend on how stressed you are to begin with?

If you were to understand that this little child is you when you are in distress, you would see that you normally admonish rather than comfort when you are upset. When distressed, you turn into a little child with little to no access to your adult higher brain centers because you are hurting or remembering a time when you were hurt. You just want to fight or fly, or be loved and have your needs met. But the big question is, what is it exactly that you need? If you knew, you probably would take care of it and not be in distress to begin with.

Exercise 3.1: Contemplation in Distress and What You Really Need

Take your time and think about your answer to each question and be as honest as you can with yourself.

Imagine you are sleep-deprived, overwhelmed with household needs, and are trying to talk on the phone with a maintenance man while massaging your head because you have a raging headache. Your kids are fighting with one another, and your spouse comes home asking what you have made for dinner.

1. How do you react?
2. Why did you react this way?
3. How do you feel about yourself after you have reacted?
4. What is it you really want and need?

I would imagine that in this scenario you might have exploded and then felt bad about yourself. Like most people, you might have also realized that what you really wanted was love, support, understanding, and to be valued.

"So what?" you might be thinking. "What good is knowing what you need if no one in your life is giving it to you?"

It is important to understand your needs so that you can find ways to take care of yourself. When you provide yourself with love and a sense of value, you do not seek it so much outside of yourself.

Most people abuse themselves with poor food choices, working long hours, not sleeping, and self-criticism. Most people, in other words, do not value themselves and suffer as a result. When you pay attention to your needs, have compassion for your own suffering, and provide yourself with the love you are seeking, you can find yourself less stressed, less attached to any given situation, less involved, and in a state of bliss more often than not.

The Healing Force of Love and Compassion

Let's take the same scenario and switch it up a bit:

Your kids are fighting, and you have a terrible headache. Your spouse comes home and has brought you a dozen roses (or your favorite bouquet of flowers) and your favorite dinner and tells you he/she just got a huge raise. Your spouse tells you to rest, take a luxurious bath, and do whatever you need to soothe your headache. You feel loved, supported, heard, and taken care of.

Do you still scream at your kids?

In this second scenario, because you are feeling more supported and loved and, therefore, balanced, you are less likely to be triggered into a rage. Even though you have a headache and your children are annoying you, you may not blow up because you are in a better state to begin with, both in mood and physiology.

The benefits of feeling loved and supported do not stop these feelings from reflecting the opposite experience of being overwhelmed and attacked. Love, as opposed to anger, fear, and other negative emotions, initiates positive emotions and a positive physiological state that opposes the negative physiology evoked by the stress response because of a release of the love hormone (oxytocin), happy chemicals like endorphins, and neurotransmitters like serotonin and dopamine. While endorphins create the sense of euphoria and relief from pain, dopamine counteracts the effects of fear and anger and improves your circulation and mood. Vasopressin and nitric oxide regulate your blood pressure and circulation, and oxytocin lowers your anxiety levels and makes you more sociable and loving. With love, stress levels are lowered along with stress hormones, memory and mood improve, wounds heal better and faster, and cardiovascular function strengthens, as does bonding, attachment, and trust that a positive future is possible.

Love also does a funny thing to your brain—it stimulates reward centers in it that make you believe anything is possible, that you are on top of the world and invincible.

Love Stimulates Happy Memories and Reward

Love induces a positive sense of reward filled with peace, balance, pleasure, and well-being. Feeling loved stimulates your memories of being happy and content. When in the state of love, your brain pulls from your positive memory bank propagating attitudes, beliefs, and emotions that are positive and well-intentioned. Your positive memory bank, like the negative, also brings forward memories, emotions, and conclusions from your past, but they are all positive. Rather than feeding you stories of negativity, victimization, and suffering, your positive memories provide you with memories of being happy, feeling good, and stories of your success.

Exercise 3.2: Noticing the Difference Between Love and Fear

A. Think about a time when you felt euphoric or full of awe—maybe you were head over heels in love, you just witnessed the most incredible sunset, or you just got back from an amazing hike in nature. Write down your experience, answering the questions that follow.

Pay attention to your chest and your breath. What happens to your breathing?

_____

_____

_____

_____

Does the chest feel open or closed? Describe what you feel.

_____

_____

_____

_____

Do you feel downcast or strong? Describe how you are feeling.

_____

_____

_____

_____

Do you feel irritated or happy? Describe the emotion.

_____

_____

_____

_____

Do you feel like you could be easily angered? Describe how close you are to falling apart and why.

_____

_____

_____

_____

B. Now think about a time when you felt humiliated, like a failure, rejected, criticized, unloved, or unwanted.

Pay attention to your chest and your breath. What happens to your breathing?

_____

_____

_____

_____

Does the chest feel open or closed? Describe what you feel.

_____

_____

_____

_____

Do you feel downcast or strong? Describe how you are feeling.

_____

_____

_____

_____

Do you feel irritated or happy? Describe the emotion.

_____

_____

_____

_____

Do you feel like you could be easily angered? Describe how close you are
to falling apart and why or why not.

_____

_____

_____

_____

_____

_____

_____

_____

I know, for one, when I am overflowing with love, or after I have hiked in nature, which often provides me with the same feelings, there is little that gets me distressed, completely in contrast to times I feel unloved, alone, or disconnected.

The problem for most of us lies in the fact that life is quite stressful and our negative emotions, conditions, and expectations are usually more prominent than the positive. Negative expectations, conditions, and emotions set off the stress response, which sets off more negative emotions, assumptions, and behaviors, which often creates a vicious cycle of negativity. We easily forget our happy memories, and unless we have continuous positive reinforcement in the form of people who love us, a life that goes the way we plan, financial abundance, and so forth, the negative memories and feelings take over.

In the state of love, you can feel secure, safe, and supported, meaning you are less likely to be or feel negatively or have an overly active stress response. You have greater access to your higher brain centers and are better able to be relaxed, evaluate your available resources and tools, access support, and solve problems. With this greater confidence and positivity, you are then more capable of attracting people who will support you, improving your reality as a result.

The key is to be able to tap into your positive memories and feelings of being loved at any point that you need to—when life is going as you plan or when it is throwing you curveballs that end up bonking you in the head.

Tapping into Love

You don't have to actually fall in love with someone to make this work. In fact, love is a physiological state that can be tapped into in a variety of ways that often have nothing to do with anyone else. You can, for instance, use your imagination to focus on the experience of being loved by someone you adore, by the universe, or by an imaginary being. Love, or the physiological state of love, can be accessed through meditation, the practice of compassion, gratitude, mindfulness, spending time in nature, volunteering, other self-care practices (like healthy eating and exercise), spirituality or spiritual activities, social support, and spending time with pets.

Exercise 3.3: Tapping into Love

A. Contemplate a situation that makes you angry. Pay particular attention to your breathing and the sensations you feel in your chest, otherwise known as your heart center.

Note your experience here:

_____

_____

_____

_____

B. Contemplate an experience of awe—a beautiful sunset, the smell of summer rain, or the look on someone's face when you surprised them with a random act of kindness. Once again, pay attention to your breathing and the sensations you experience in your body, particularly your heart center. Continue to focus on this experience of awe for another moment or two, enjoying it as much as you can.

Note your experience here:

_____

_____

_____

_____

C. Think about the situation that makes you angry again. This time, note if there is a change from the first experience as well as the second. Did your chest close, open, close again? Was it as bad the second time, after being in the state of love for a moment or two?

Note your experience here:

_____

_____

_____

_____

You may have noted that your chest tightened up and your breaths became shorter and more constricted when you were distressed. You may also have noticed that your chest opened up and your breaths lengthened when contemplating a loving experience. In the latter case, did you notice though that the restricted feeling in your chest was not as strong as the first time around when contemplating the upsetting thought again?

Just like that, within seconds, you changed your physiological response by tapping into the physiology of love, which I called The Love Response[®4] many years ago. Tapping into love on a regular basis can influence every part of your life. This can include healing old hurts and negative stories, quickly shifting out of a negative mood and accessing your higher brain centers, taking better care of yourself and making stronger life choices, having more loving relationships, and being a happier and healthier person.

The TMI Process to Using Love

More often than not, tapping into the physiology of love will help you find your bliss as you are able to keep the stress response under control, your mood and your beliefs positive, and your reactions strong and calm. The process involves bringing love into your life in three action steps:

1. Use love to resolve underlying hurts and negative beliefs or stories that you have held onto for a long time.
2. Shift into the physiology of love to get out of a negative mood, as this lower mood diminishes your trigger threshold.
3. Create more love and support in your life by getting more sleep, eating healthier, joining a support group, and so forth.

To help you remember what you need to do and how to then apply love, you can use the acronym TMI:

T = Trigger assessment and resolution
M = Mood assessment and shifting
I = Infrastructure assessment and rebuilding

Action Step 1: Trigger Assessment and Resolution

You only get triggered if there is something there to be triggered by. No one can make you feel inferior or disrespected if you already believe in and know your own greatness and value. For instance, someone may act rudely toward you or cut you off in line while waiting for a coffee. This person has certainly disrespected you, which is unpleasant and irritating. But is this a cause for explosion? If your reaction outweighs the severity of the situation, it is safe to bet that somewhere inside you there exists a memory of being disrespected and devalued. It is now up to you to find that memory, heal it, and forever be un-triggered.

To assess your trigger, you will want to refer to your Distress Assessment Chart, and follow the four steps necessary to create your categories of distress:

1. Validate your feelings, acknowledging to yourself that you have the right to feel distress.

2. Witness your physiology by taking note of your physical and emotional reaction—what you feel in your body, where you feel the tension, and what emotions are rising up in you.

3. Label the reason you are distressed, asking yourself why you feel the way you do.

4. Notice how you express and react.

Distress Assessment Chart

What happened?	What is my physical reaction?	How is it making me feel?	How do I react?	What can I do to heal?	What is my new response?
Unsupported					
Ignored					
Rejection					
Humiliation					
Injustice					
Disappointment					
Grief/loss					
Illness/pain					

Assessing your trigger will also involve asking yourself if your reaction is appropriate, over-the-top, or one that caused you to feel bad about yourself. If you don't like the way you feel or how you behaved, or if you note that you have blown up when you want to be blissing out, start asking yourself these questions that will help you to further label your feelings and the situation and know if you have been triggered.

Trigger Questions

- Do I feel triggered? Y/N
- Am I angrier than what the situation calls for? Y/N
- Do I feel out of control? Y/N
- Am I acting in the same way I always have when really angry? Y/N
- Is this experience leading me to feel more negatively about myself? Y/N
- When have I felt this feeling before? Y/N
- Is the feeling or belief that I have right now even true? Y/N
- Is the feeling or belief that I have right now even logical? Y/N

If you have uncovered that you are overreacting, expressing your distress in an unhealthy way, or feeling bad about yourself, you can assume, of course, that you have been triggered. In addition, asking yourself if your belief is true or logical will help guide you to the memory that your brain is tapping into. The more negative the belief, the more illogical and untrue it usually is. You can tell a negative, false belief from a true, logical, or positive one by paying attention to descriptive words like "always," "never," "no one," or "everyone." Examples of thoughts or stories that are likely untrue, illogical, and negative are contained in the list below.

Examples of untrue, false, and illogical statements

- No one loves me.
- I always get treated this way.
- I never get what I want.
- He always does this to me.
- No one values my contribution.
- I always have to do everything myself.
- No one listens to me.

Action Step 2: Mood Assessment and Shifting

The mood you are in shapes your perception of any given situation. Wake up on the wrong side of the bed? Most things will irritate you. You feel lucky? Very little will get your goat. A negative state of mind breeds negative physiology, which gives your amygdala more power. A positive mindset gives you power over the amygdala as you have more access to higher brain centers, including your prefrontal cortex, positive thinking, and reward circuits.

Assessing your mood is pretty self-explanatory—Do you feel good or bad? Happy or sad? Negative or positive? You simply need to observe what and how you are feeling and have been feeling emotionally and physically. Also ask yourself the following questions when you find yourself triggered and relate it back to your Distress Assessment Chart:

- Was my stress response highly active prior to this incident? Y/N
- Was I in a good mood or bad? Y/N
- Was I happy, sad, annoyed, tired, overwhelmed, or indifferent? Circle the descriptions that apply.
- Have I been feeling like a victim lately? Y/N
- Have I been feeling lucky or unlucky? Lucky/Unlucky
- Do I perceive the world as a good place or a bad place right now? Good/Bad
- Have I been upset about anything recently that I am not addressing? Y/N
- If I answered yes to being upset, what have I been upset about? Describe.

_____

_____

_____

Action Step 3: Infrastructure Assessment and Rebuilding

If you are feeling sick, sleep-deprived, overwhelmed, overburdened, unsatisfied with your life, or have been eating poorly and not getting the exercise or exposure to nature that your body needs, not only are you more likely to be unhappy and in a bad mood, but you are more apt to get triggered. Sleep, good nutrition, movement, spending time in nature, social support, spirituality, meditation, and counseling are all examples of what I term "infrastructure," a system of support for your mind, body, and life. Having a solid infrastructure keeps your stress response in check and you happy and healthy. You can ask yourself these questions when you are angry or even on an ongoing basis:

Have I been running on empty? Y/N
If yes, describe.

_____

_____

_____

Have I had enough sleep? Y/N
If no, describe.

_____

_____

_____

Do I feel rested or tired? Rested/Tired
Describe.

_____

_____

_____

Am I in any pain? Y/N
If yes, describe.

_____

_____

_____

Is there a physical reason I am more irritable? Y/N
If yes, describe.

_____

_____

_____

Do I feel that I am lacking in support from other people? Y/N
If yes, describe.

_____

_____

_____

What else is bothering me in my life? Describe.

_____

_____

_____

When is the last time I felt connected to something bigger than just my little life? Describe.

_____

_____

_____

Do I feel alone? Y/N
If yes, describe.

_____

_____

_____

When is the last time I did something fun or playful? Describe.

_____

_____

_____

When is the last time I spent time in nature? Describe.

_____

_____

_____

When is the last time I exercised? Describe.

_____

_____

_____

What have I been eating over the past few days? Describe.

_____

_____

_____

I often compare a good infrastructure to a strong dam that has several outlets for water to be released. Imagine, if you will, that this dam is your life and that it is constantly being filled by rain, which is akin to the stress in your life. If you have no outlets for the water, the dam will eventually overflow and break. With outlets for release, the water can stay level and the dam strong. When your infrastructure is intact, you make sure that you have several outlets to keep your stress in check and taken care of. A strong infrastructure has everything to do with loving your-self enough to take care of yourself, connecting with others who can love and support you and to something larger than you that helps you get by, like nature or a spiritual belief.

In the next chapter, you will learn about creating a solid infrastructure or how to strengthen the one you have. For now, I encourage you to fill out the following questionnaire to assess where you stand with regard to your TMI to give you an idea of where you have some work to do. Know that these questions are not meant to make you feel bad or guilty. Rather, this exercise prepares you for the all-important first step in your healing process: becoming aware of what is going well in your life and what still needs work.

Exercise 3.4: The TMI Questionnaire

Please rate the following questions as follows:

- Always true = 4
- More times than not = 3
- Rarely true = 2
- Not true = 1

When you are done, simply add up your score.

- A score of 160 means you may not need to read this book, but read it anyway because you are curious.
- A score of 120–159 means you could use this book for light reading and learn a bit.
- A score of 80–119 means it's probably a good idea for you to take good notes and implement some changes.
- If your score is 30–79, it means you might want to have your highlighter ready as you may need to read this book a few times over as you continue to make life changes.

Aside from your total score, take note of which categories are the most problematic for you. Take your time and answer the following questions as truthfully and honestly as you can.

Social support

1. I feel I am respected and loved by my significant other.
2. My personal relationships are nurturing, rather than tense and melodramatic.
3. I feel that I can count on my friends or family to support me at any time.
4. I don't take on tasks all by myself often as I know how to ask for help and delegate responsibilities well to others.
5. I rarely get angry or upset with my friends or loved ones.
6. I enjoy spending time doing things with other people and do so frequently.

Work support

7. I feel I am respected and supported by my colleagues.
8. My work relationships are more often congenial rather than tense and stressful.
9. I have adequate support at work and feel that I can express my needs and be heard.

Self-love/value

10. I feel complete within myself, never needing to reward myself with food or alcohol after having a hard day.
11. I value my own company and enjoy spending time alone.
12. I feel secure with myself and know my own value.
13. I am honest and loving with myself about my faults and imperfections.
14. I am good at making myself happy and giving myself the things I need.

Self and physical care/health

15. I am good at making sure I get regular exercise.
16. I always feel rested when I wake up in the morning.
17. I make sure I get adequate sleep more often than not.
18. I rarely eat sugar, bad fats, or processed foods as my diet consists of vegetables, some fruit, protein, and healthy fats.

19. I feel physically very healthy and rarely experience pain or other symptoms.

Acceptance and expression

20. I am honest and loving with others about their faults and imperfections.

21. I am able to express how I feel calmly.

22. If I don't express myself calmly and lose my temper, I can do so without also having feelings of shame or guilt.

23. I do not cast blame on myself when something goes wrong.

24. I do not cast blame on others when something goes wrong.

Criticism and accountability

25. I can take criticism without falling apart.

26. I feel that for the most part, I have been treated fairly in my life and circumstances that befall me are usually fair.

27. I can offer criticism with compassion and without being hurtful.

28. I can listen without getting angry or upset when I am being criticized.

29. I am able to take risks as I never fear of rejection.

30. I am able to let go of disappointing or hurtful situations without ruminating or constantly feeling a sense of loss or grief.

Spirituality

31. I have a spiritual belief system and/or feel connected to nature, God, or Spirit.

32. I often take walks or engage in activities out in nature.

33. I often volunteer my time or efforts to help others.

34. I feel like I belong to some kind of community, one made up of friends or other people who share my interests, such as a spiritual or religious belief system or love of a sport or hobby.

35. I know how to remain calm and find time to relax or meditate.

36. I feel like I have a life purpose.

Sense of humor

37. I enjoy laughing often.

38. I can make a fool of myself and laugh and not feel humiliated.

39. I have a hobby or passion that I am actively involved with that brings me joy.

40. I think that my imperfections make me who I am, and I can laugh at myself and take myself less seriously.

Total Score _____

Zapping Stress with Love

Knowing that you have been triggered tells you that the child in you is having a tantrum and is in need of soothing with compassion and care. Through the course of this book, you will discover a variety of tools that will allow you to heal your trigger, change your mood, and fix your infrastructure. You will learn to use your imagination, use affirmations, or take part in activities that support the experience of feeling more loved and valued. You will discover how to switch your mood and mindset from negative to positive pretty much any time by redirecting your focus to another thought or memory, finding your humor button, or doing something loving and generous for yourself or others to break your mood.

Ready for more? Let's move on to really looking and fixing your infrastructure.

Chapter 4
Restructure Your Infrastructure

....

"It is wise to direct your anger towards problems—not people; to focus your energies on answers—not excuses."

—William Arthur Ward

If you haven't figured it out yet, your brain is not separate from your body and neither are separate from your environment. This means that what you put in your body, do with your body, and surround yourself with in your life will affect how you feel, how you think, how you perceive yourself in your world—enough or not enough—and ultimately how you react. A balanced life translates to a more balanced you.

You might be thinking to yourself, "A balanced life? I have no time for that! If I had time to be balanced, I wouldn't be reading this book!"

And you could be absolutely right. Having said that, you can always create balance in your life, even if you do not have time. It may mean making a few changes within the time you have to get the stress response under control in as many ways as possible so that you don't find yourself so easily triggered. Keep in mind that the more you abuse yourself with poor lifestyle habits, the more you will perceive the world as abusive, take things personally, and feel more stressed.

I know, for example, that when I eat foods that are processed or high in sugar, I feel more depressed and anxious the following day. I have less patience, am more irritable, and my negative stories play more prominently in my head. The same is true when I don't get enough sleep.

Have you filled out the questionnaire? What parts of your life or infrastructure need help? In this chapter, I will review what I believe are the important aspects of the infrastructure that you can build to help you keep calm, feel better, and find more bliss.

Munchies to Turn Your Moody to Merry: Nutrition

You've heard the saying "You are what you eat." It's true, for the most part. If you eat junk, you will feel like junk. If you eat healthy, nurturing foods, you will feel the same. In which state do you imagine you are more prone to be triggered to be stressed?

Your brain is functioning 24/7 and needs to be supported with high-grade fuel, much of which comes from the foods you eat. The fuel you take in greatly influences the structure and function of your brain and your mood. Like an expensive car, your brain works best on premium fuel that comes from foods that contain loads of vitamins, minerals, antioxidants, proteins, complex carbohydrates, and good fats, which nourish the brain and protect it from being damaged.

When you ingest anything but premium fuel, your brain suffers. Low premium fuels such as refined sugars, trans fats, processed foods, and chemicals can harm the brain because they promote inflammation, have negative influences on insulin, and cause oxidative stress, which is essentially a process of rusting. Science is showing us now that a diet high in refined sugars, for instance, can worsen mood disorders, including depression.[5]

One of the reasons this happens is because a poor diet will cause your serotonin levels to fall. Serotonin is a neurotransmitter that helps regulate sleep, appetite, pain, and mood. About 95 percent of your serotonin is produced in your gut, which is lined with millions of nerve cells that are directly wired to your brain. (This is why when you are nervous, you may experience butterflies in your belly.) In the lining of your gut, you also have friendly bacteria that help digest and absorb nutrients, protect you from toxins and inflammation, and influence the production of neurotransmitters, like serotonin.

When you eat poorly, as with the typical Western diet, not only do you take in foods that are void of the nutrients required to make neurotransmitters and fuel your brain, but you are also ingesting foods that cause inflammation, "rusting," damage to the good bacteria, and more stress on your body. More stress causes the stress hormone, cortisol, to rise, which can cause a further drop in levels of absorbed vitamins and minerals, including the B vitamins, which normally influence mood positively. As inflammation runs rampant through your body and necessary vitamin and neurotransmitters fall, your mood does too.

I encourage you to start paying attention to how eating different foods makes you feel—not just in the moment, but the next day. The junkier your diet, the junkier your brain will feel. Even though you may crave comfort food when you are down, many of the foods you choose are not comforting to your brain and are therefore not helping you in the least, neither your health nor your mood. The best way to really pay attention is to keep a log of your nutrition intake, along with your mood changes, up or down.

Exercise 4.1: Nutrition/Mood Log

You can use the following sample log to keep track of how you feel within twenty-four hours after eating, taking special attention to experiences when eating dairy, sugar, baked goods, and processed foods of any kind. Note any symptoms you might experience such as irritability, anxiety, poor sleep, heartburn, indigestion, change in bowel habits, headaches, congestion, poor concentration, "fuzzy" thinking, and so forth, along with signs of feeling good, energized, pain-free, and so forth. You may also want to note the severity of the symptoms and the timing (within an hour of eating or somewhere within the twenty-four-hour period). Additional information can include how the food was prepared, who prepared it (you or a restaurant, for instance), and brand.

Nutrition/Mood Log

Food	Quantity	Time of day eaten	Time of symptom	Symptom and notes

As you keep this log, try to eat a "clean" diet for three weeks. This involves cutting out all processed foods and sugar and eating lots of vegetables, a couple of pieces of fruit a day, grass-fed and hormone-free protein, and some nuts and seeds, healthy fats like avocado, cold-pressed olive oil and coconut oil, and gluten-free grains like quinoa. Add fermented foods like kimchi, miso, sauerkraut, pickles, or kombucha or probiotic foods to get those friendly bacteria in and working. You also might want to try going dairy free as well as grain free. Note how you feel.

After three weeks, slowly introduce foods back into your diet, one by one, and keep track of any changes that may occur. Many of you may have food sensitivities that you are not aware of that may be setting off an inflammatory response, which shows up physically in you as irritability and change in mood. The more in tune you are with yourself, the more power you have in helping yourself to feel happy and healthy.

It is also important for you not to skip meals. A drop in blood sugar may cause you to become more irritable. If you are someone who typically does tend to become "hangry" (hungry angry), try to eat five to six small meals a day to keep up your blood sugar level.

The Bottom Line for Nutrition and Mood

- Keep a daily log.
- Avoid refined sugar (especially high-fructose corn syrup), processed foods, and white flour products.
- Avoid deep fried foods and foods made with hydrogenated oils and trans fats.
- Eat plenty of vegetables, two pieces of fruit, lean and hormone-free proteins, some nuts and seeds daily, and healthy fats, keeping your grains to a minimum.
- Try to stick to the 80/20 rule—Eighty percent clean and 20 percent whatever you want, always keeping track of how different foods may affect your mood.

- If you would like to cleanse your system and get more specific guidance and kick-start your body into a healthy you, you may want to try my seven-day filter diet (see www.drselhub.com).

Move It or Lose It: Exercise

I cannot stress enough how important exercise and movement are to keep your mood balanced. Keep in mind that humans were not meant to be sedentary. We roamed the earth, looking for shelter, scavenging, finding food, and building forts. The term "survival of the fittest" should tell you that being a couch potato is not conducive to the survival of the species. Being sedentary is also not conducive to maintaining a happy mood.

Exercise not only offers a myriad of health benefits, but it also helps control the stress response and aids in raising serotonin and endorphin levels, which stabilize mood.[6] Even if infrequently done, exercise can have a positive effect against the building up of anger. Exercising when you are angry, for example, gives you the opportunity to release pent-up energy and have a chance to think. I will review a variety of techniques in Chapter 7 that will enable you to diffuse stress through the use of different types of movement that give you the opportunity to both exercise and resolve internal conflict.

As a general rule, I do recommend you get your butt off the couch and get your body moving. Not only will your brain and body thank you physiologically, but you will feel much better about yourself. The more you value yourself, the less you will be triggered by other people's actions.

Exercise 4.2: Activity and Exercise Prescription

The best prescription for exercise is finding something you enjoy and stick to it. You want to mix it up with two to three days of shorter and more intense strength-training workouts, and active rest days where you partake in low-intensity movement like walking, hiking, or taking a slow bike ride or swim. Strength-training workouts do not need to involve weights, if you prefer not to use them, as you can use your own body weight. Movements can include push-ups, pull-ups, squats, planks, etc. These types of exercises help you build lean muscle mass, strengthen your bones, improve your metabolism, and help you be stronger (not just feel it). You may opt for yoga, Pilates, jogging, biking, or swimming. There are no rights or wrongs. Keeping a log of your weekly activities and observing how you feel, positively or negatively, will also help you hone in on the activities that best suit you and a happy mood.

Below is an example of what you can do during the week for exercise and how to keep a log.

Sample Exercise Week

Day 1: Walk at a moderate pace with a friend for thirty minutes at 75 percent of max heart rate.

Day 2: Twenty-five-minute strength training.

Day 3: Zumba class or go hiking at fast pace aiming for a sprint workout. You can try cycling on a stationary bike, running sprints, rowing on an erg, etc.

Day 4: Active rest, walk your dog or someone else's dog (effort about 55 percent of max heart rate) for an hour.

Day 5: Twenty-five-minute strength training.

Day 6: Walk outdoors with a friend for thirty minutes at 75 percent of max heart rate.

Day 7: Active rest, walk your dog or someone else's dog (effort about 55 percent of max heart rate) for an hour.

Activity/Mood Log

Day	Type of activity	Time of day	Mood before	Mood after
Monday				
Tuesday				
Wednesday				
Thursday				
Friday				
Saturday				
Sunday				

The Bottom Line for Exercise

- Keep a daily log of activities. You may consider getting a Fitbit or other type of monitor that shows you the effects of your efforts on your pulse, breathing, and sleep.
- Have fun or else you may get bored and stop exercising.
- Find friends or an exercise buddy, who may also be able to help talk you through your problems.
- Exercise outdoors, as you are more likely to enjoy the workout and have less discomfort or fatigue.

Who's Got Your Back? Social Support

As social beings, humans desire to be in groups, as the support we get is crucial to our health and well-being. Largely due to the release of the hormone oxytocin and the drop in stress hormones, social support helps us feel better, cope, and be healthier, especially if the relationships are strong and loving.[7]

The key words here are "strong and loving," because when the love between you and others is strong, it sustains you and gives your life reason and meaning. It reminds you that you are valued and worthy, which helps keep your sense of Self intact and mind at peace. This love enables you to feel safer and more secure. It stimulates your personal growth and identity and helps you manage life's hardships, ultimately keeping your stress response in check and your mood more in control.

For most of you who have distress switches that tend to be turned on quite often, it may be that you are lacking in such love in your life. It may be, in fact, that the reason you feel stressed so often is that the relationships in your life are not supportive or loving enough, or at least you do not perceive them as such. If you are in relationships that are not loving, supportive, or as giving as they are receiving, you will be triggered into distress frequently. The lack of love, in other words, is the reason you feel bad in the first place.

When assessing the social support part of your infrastructure, therefore, you want to analyze how supportive people are in your life and also how good you are when it comes to receiving support. If you are incapable of asking for help and receiving it, the problem may not lie with the other person, but with you not feeling worthy of being loved or knowing how to ask.

Exercise 4.3: Ability to Receive Self-Assessment

A. Statements: Circle true or false

- I find it hard to say no to people. True/False
- I often feel it is my responsibility to make sure everyone is happy. True/False
- I feel it reflects badly on me if I don't make other people happy. True/False
- I am the one always listening to other people's problems but rarely telling them about my own. True/False
- I have a hard time asking for what I need. True/False

If you answered "true" for two or more of these statements, it is likely that you tend to give rather than receive love and support, which means you may more easily find yourself tapped out, overwhelmed, and resentful. The question you may want to ask yourself, then, is:

B. Questions: Why do I give and not receive? What am I scared of? Take your time to think about and write your answer, particularly focusing on what you might be scared of if you say no or fail to give and make others happy. Think about what might happen as a result of your actions. I would suggest taking each of the statements in A and figuring out what fear may be behind your answer.

_____

_____

_____

_____

_____

_____

_____

_____

Once you have assessed why you may be more likely to give or receive, take a closer look at your actual relationships. Who gives to you? Who takes? Who boosts you up, and who shuts you down? Once you have answered these questions, see if your fears (your answers to B) play a role in the dynamics of the relationship by assessing your relationships using the following guide.

Exercise 4.4: Relationships Assessment

Soul Family Assessment Log

Relationship	Gives to me	Receives from me	Boosts my sense of Self	Hurts my sense of Self	My role in the dynamic
Mother					
Father					
Sibling					
Friend					
Coworker					

Is your life void of support, or is it not as bad as you thought? What role are you or your fears playing? In many cases, working on letting go of your own fears can change the dynamics of your relationships, creating more balance, shared love, and support. Throughout this book, you will learn how to rid yourself of your fears and discover your own self-value, which will enable you to create more balanced relationships.

Sometimes, no matter what you do, the relationship will never be balanced. In such cases, it may be necessary for you to distance yourself from the person or end the relationship altogether. No matter the situation, I encourage you to enhance your life with relationships that do feed you in order to handle the ones that don't. You can do so by going to places or doing activities where you have shared interests with people. I suggest joining a local church, synagogue, spiritual organization or group (it could be a meditation group), or other interest groups like a book club, knitting group, hiking or movie club, and so forth. The key is for you to engage with others who share interests with you and to eventually feel like you belong to something or someone. The more you feel like you belong, the stronger you will feel internally and the less triggered you will be when under stress.

Bottom Line for Social Support

- Understand what it takes for you to feel good (more sleep, healthy food, intimate conversation, someone actually listening to you, a hug, and so forth).
- Once you are clear about what you might need at any given moment, choose the right people who will be able to help you with those needs (you don't go to a car mechanic to fix your broken leg).
- Practice asking for help.
- Practice letting people know that sometimes you just want to be heard, not told what to do.
- Set an intention to check in with a friend or loved one daily, by phone or in person. You may want to create an agreement with them on when this check-in can happen.
- Make play dates at least once a week with someone you would like to get to know better or whose relationship you want to nurture.
- Join a club, support group, spiritual/religious group, or community that shares your interests.

Finding Oneness: Spirituality

Feeling like you belong doesn't just involve finding people to be with you but also connecting to something larger than just you or connecting to your spirituality. Being spiritual is not about being religious, believing in God, or even praying. It is about sharing, giving, and receiving love from something that is beyond you, what you see, and what is in front of you. It is about faith.

Faith helps you get through hard situations, understand that you are not alone, and find meaning. The more meaning you have in your life, the less helpless you feel in adverse circumstances and the more valued you feel in general. Though I am not advocating that you become religious, I am suggesting that if there is something that you feel drawn to—a particular religious or spiritual belief, process, nature, or purpose—then make the time to get involved with it so that you can work on building your faith in something greater that supports you.

A simple way to get started is by regularly connecting to your sense of awe. You can do so by admiring a beautiful sunset or other aspects of nature and making a concerted effort to notice small miracles happening around you. You can develop a meditation practice as well, which has the effect of lowering your stress response and giving you access to happy chemicals that induce a sense of calm and peace within you.

Your meditation practice does not need to involve sitting in lotus position and chanting "ohm" for hours on end. There are many different techniques you can try out, including mindfulness meditation, yoga, tai chi, progressive muscle relaxation, guided meditation, mantra meditation, mindful walks in nature, and so forth. The key is to create a sacred, quiet place to sit, walk, or lie down where you can be comfortable (but not sleep), find a focus to concentrate on—like an image, word, prayer, phrase, object of beauty and awe (like nature), or movement—assume a nonjudgmental attitude, and let your daily thoughts float away.

Bottom Line for Spirituality

- Join a church, synagogue, Buddhist temple, or another type of religious or spiritual community that you resonate with.
- Create a daily ritual of prayer and gratitude when starting your day, eating your evening meal, and/or going to bed.
- Take five to twenty minutes a day to close your eyes and take deep breaths as you contemplate an experience of awe.
- Keep a miracle journal, where you keep a daily log of the things you feel grateful for in your life and the little miracles that you witness.
- Develop a meditation practice (you will get tips about this throughout the book).
- Spend more time in nature.

Choose Nature over Screen-Time

As a society, we have become addicted to the screen. Perusing the information highway on the smartphone or computer has displaced exercise, meaningful social interaction, healthy eating, and getting appropriate amounts of sleep. Researchers have found that there is a strong connection between screen time and higher rates of depression, anxiety, poor performance, and lack of empathy.[8] What this translates to is more stress, less patience, and meaner people.

If you want to stay as one of the statistics, go right ahead and be miserable. But if you want to find bliss, you may want to get off your screen and get back into nature. In fact, science is showing us now that nature does reduce stress hormones and improve immunity.[9]

Twenty minutes is all you need, but the more, the better. Work in the garden, walk in a park, visit the ocean, or rest while lying on the ground after a picnic. Take your pick. The key is to spend time being in nature, feeling nature, seeing nature, eating nature, and yes, smelling nature. If you do, you will feel calmer and less angry. It also counts as a spiritual activity, so I encourage you to mark your nature experiences in your daily log of activities/mood.

In essence, you want to immerse yourself and all your senses in the experience of nature. Smell, sense, taste, listen, look, and enjoy the wonders around you. Aside from turning your mind off of your daily stresses, you will also get exposed to nature's healing chemicals called phytoncides—chemicals that get to your brain through your nose that stimulate or relax your brain and may even benefit your immune system as they lower your stress response.[10] In short, immersing yourself in nature helps your brain shift into a positive mental state, turn off the stress response, and feel more connected spiritually.

Bottom Line for Nature

- Take a twenty-minute walk in nature.
- Exercise outdoors.
- Garden indoors or out.

- Put a plant in your office and consider having photos of nature as well.
- Take a few minutes out of your hectic day to close your eyes and imagine yourself luxuriating somewhere in nature.
- Spend the day at the beach.
- Get away for a weekend or week to nature, be it on your own or on a wellness retreat.

In your Activity/Mood Log, jot down such activities as being out in nature, meditation, or being on the screen, and note how your mood is affected, positively or negatively. You may choose to exercise outdoors, which will have a double positive effect on your health and mood. See if it does!

Exercise 4.5: Activity/Mood Log

Activity/Mood Log

Day	Type of activity	Time of day	Mood before	Mood after
Monday				
Tuesday				
Wednesday				
Thursday				
Friday				
Saturday				
Sunday				

Getting Your Zzzz's: Sleep

Lack of sleep has negative consequences on almost every aspect of your health and your life. It wreaks havoc on your immune system, hormones, muscle and bone mass, brain function, heart, and weight. Did you know that studies show that people who sleep less than six hours a day have a much higher risk of becoming obese than those who sleep seven to nine hours?[11] This may not seem relevant to you, but not being able to lose weight is a big reason many of my patients get upset. If you are like these patients, you get frustrated when the scale doesn't change or goes up. You get mad at your body and yourself and are short-tempered with people who are close to you. You feel worse about yourself and stuff your face because your lack of sleep is causing your food cravings to skyrocket.

Getting more than seven and a half hours of sleep can stop that cycle, even if you don't get that sleep all at once but through the accumulation of a nap or two during the day. The question is, why aren't you getting adequate sleep? Does your partner snore? Do you snore? If you do snore loudly and sometimes wake yourself up with a snort, you may have sleep apnea, which occurs when your airways get blocked while you sleep. This can be a serious condition, so check with your doctor, who can provide you with a remedy. It's worth it. Trust me.

What could other reasons be? Do you have a hard time falling or staying asleep? How much caffeine are you drinking? Are you inputting too much stimulus at night with electronics, work, or television? Do you have a hard time winding down?

You do not have to live your life sleep deprived and angry, so it behooves you to assess your sleep, along with your mood, and to match it up with the other logs. You may note that when you eat better, exercise, and connect with your spirituality, you sleep better. In the remarks section, write in notes that may have affected your sleep or symptoms you may have experienced that did. You can, for instance, write about food cravings, if you felt more stressed, had pain or other physical complaints when trying to sleep, and so forth.

Exercise 4.6: Sleep Assessment Log

Sleep Assessment Log

Day	Hours slept night prior	Times waking up through night	Felt rested in a.m. (y/n)	Mood	Remarks
Monday					
Tuesday					
Wednesday					
Thursday					
Friday					
Saturday					
Sunday					

Bottom Line for Sleep

- Try meditation prior to sleep or other relaxation techniques like progressive muscle relaxation: starting with the soles of your feet and moving through to your head, tense each muscle group for five seconds and then allow those muscle to relax for thirty seconds.
- Do not bring electronics to the bedroom, especially work or anything that acts as a stimulus to your brain.
- Use your bed only for sleep or sex.
- Keep the bedroom atmosphere quiet, dark, and at a comfortable temperature.
- Avoid fluids after 8:00 p.m. so that you are not awakened to go to the bathroom.

- Avoid large or heavy meals prior to bedtime.
- Avoid foods and drinks containing caffeine, sugar, or alcohol.
- Consider taking supplements like magnesium to naturally promote relaxation.
- Exercise regularly during the earlier hours of the day as this will also help regulate cortisol and other hormone levels, which will help you sleep better.
- Assess your bed as it may be that your bed is uncomfortable for your body and preventing you from being able to fully relax.
- Kick your partner out of the room until he or she takes care of their snoring problem.
- If you continue to feel tired when you awaken in the morning despite getting more than seven or eight hours of sleep, consider seeing your doctor for a sleep study to make sure you do not have some underlying condition like sleep apnea that can be taken care of.

As you work on building your infrastructure, you will likely notice that you feel lighter, happier, more rested, more fulfilled, and ultimately, less angry.

Chapter 5
Melt Your Mood with Meditation

....

"The best fighter is never angry."

—Lao Tzu

Though you may still be holding on to the belief that stress is "bad," I encourage you to remember that stress is a powerful force that can motivate you into action and empower you. Stress is therefore not inherently bad, but rather is an energy that needs to be used for positive action. What is usually bad is not the stress itself but the action or reaction that stems from it. As I have explained, the reaction occurs as a result of an intense emotional trigger. The key is to learn how to detach yourself from the intense emotion, like a peaceful warrior, so that you can use the energy of stress to motivate you to look deeper into a problem, find solutions, communicate effectively, become more creative, and invent new ideas.

How can you transform yourself into a peaceful warrior when your instincts push you to be a raving lunatic?

You learn how to get centered so that when you are triggered or faced with a stressful situation, you can maintain your cool. Learning to get centered usually means developing some sort of meditation practice, one where you train yourself to empty your mind of the rambling negative thoughts, cue your body's muscles to relax, deepen your breaths, and detach from your emotions and life circumstances.

More on Meditation

For many of you, the idea of meditating may sound foreign and hard. Perhaps you believe meditation involves sitting in lotus position and chanting "ohm" for hours on end. Though doing so will enable you to achieve a meditative state over time, you don't have to chant or sit like a pretzel to meditate. There are many ways to meditate, and even better, there is no right or wrong in what you choose to do. There is simply you doing it or trying to, which is better than screaming at someone else or eating a pint of ice cream.

When you meditate, your body shifts into a physiological response, which is the mirror opposite to the stress response. In 1971, Dr. Herbert Benson studied the physiological changes when his study participants practiced transcendental meditation and coined the physiological changes that occurred during their practice as the "relaxation response." He later discovered that the relaxation response occurred during a variety of forms of meditation, including (but not limited to) yoga, prayer, mindfulness meditation, progressive muscle relaxation, and self-hypnosis. The common denominator, he found, was that this response reflected a state of deep rest brought about by focused attention on a simple mental stimulus such as a word, phrase, or image, for example, "In peace, out tension," "Ohm," or a prayer, like "The Lord is my shepherd . . ."

Dr. Benson's research, along with many other studies performed over the past fifty years all over the world, has shown that elicitation of the relaxation response can lower heart rate, blood pressure, metabolic rate, respiratory rate, and muscle tension.[12] It can improve sleep, lower the need for medications, reduce pain, lower levels of anxiety and depression, and reduce symptoms associated with premenstrual syndrome.[13] The list is endless.

What is really interesting to me is how the response affects the brain. EEG studies, for instance, show that people who practice the relaxation response exhibit a slow synchronization of alpha and theta brain waves. Alpha waves are related with a state of relaxed wakefulness and allow you to be creative and open and understand new concepts. When you meditate, alpha wave synchronization occurs, which means your ability to be creative, think clearly, and take in new ideas improves.[14] The opposite occurs with emotional tension: alpha waves are blocked. Theta activity is usually associated with processes that link your higher brain centers together, like the cortex and hypothalamus, enabling mature thinking and emotional processing, deep insights, and alignment with your intuition. Theta waves are also blocked when under duress.

The point here is that the calmer and quieter your mind and body are, the more access you have to your intelligence and intuition. In this state, you make better choices, find better words to express yourself, and are more creative about finding suitable solutions. Even more so, in this state, you care without caring. In other words, you lose your emotional attachment to any given situation and are able to observe it with detached openness and compassion instead.

You can see for yourself how stress and relaxation affect your ability to think clearly by doing the following exercise.

Exercise 5.1: Assessment of Tension

Think about a person or a situation that you are angry or upset about. Really let the tension rise up in your body and into your brain. Let yourself get upset. Think about the person or situation, ask yourself these questions, and write down your answers. Try not to think too much about your answers and instead write freely without holding back. Let the words flow on paper.

What do I want to do to this person or situation?

_____

_____

_____

_____

Do I feel like there is a solution?

_____

_____

_____

_____

Do I feel in or out of control of the situation?

_____

_____

_____

_____

If I were to pick up the phone and call this person or even run into him or her right now, how would I react?

_____

_____

_____

_____

What am I doing with my breaths?

_____

_____

_____

_____

How does my body feel? Am I tense? Where am I holding this tension?

_____

_____

_____

_____

As you examine your thoughts, reactions, breath, and your body's state of tension, take note of how in control or out of control you might feel. Did you notice that you held your breath or took very shallow breaths? Both feeling out of control and not really breathing send messages to your brain that you are under threat, causing your stress response to fire.

To bring this point home, I'd like you to do the next exercise that will show you how your physical tension affects your mental state and how your mental tension affects your physical state.

Exercise 5.2: Physical Tension Creates Mental Tension

Continue to think about a person or a situation that you are angry or upset about. As you do so, make a fist and punch the air as if you are punching someone.

- Keeping one fist clenched and your focus on your anger, clench the other fist and bring both fists close to you as if you are ready to punch someone.
- Now try and think of a solution.
- Take note of what comes to mind and how tense your body feels.

Are you able to think clearly? Describe your experience.

_____

_____

_____

_____

_____

_____

_____

You may note that after you punch the air (or someone), you do feel better, but it is probably better to feel a release and less tense without inflicting harm on someone else. You can shift out of tension quite easily, using your breath.

Exercise 5.3: Shifting out of Tension with Power Breaths

Resume your focus on being angry and continue to tighten your fists. Now redirect your attention away from the subject of your anger and focus on your breath.

- Breathe in slowly and count 1-2-3-4.
- Then exhale slowly, letting all the air out of your lungs, counting 1-2-3-4-5.
- Do it again. Breathe in on the count of four and breathe out on the count of five.
- On the third breath, imagine that all the thoughts in your head float away down a river, into the wind, or up to the stars.
- Breathe in, count to four.
- Breathe out, count to five, letting all your thoughts and tension flow out of your mind and body down the river, into the wind, or up to the stars.
- Breathe in, count to four.
- Breathe out, count to five, letting all your thoughts and tension flow out.
- Breathe in, count to four, and breathe in peace and love.
- Breathe out, count to five, and empty your mind and relax your body.
- Breathe in, count to four, and breathe in peace and love.
- Breathe out, count to five, and empty your mind and relax your body.

Take a few minutes now to note how you feel, both in your body and about the situation. Do you feel differently? Do you care as much? Is there a possible solution? Write freely as thoughts and realizations arise.

_____

_____

_____

_____

_____

You can practice this cycle of breathing for as long as you wish, paying close attention to how much more relaxed and at ease you feel over time. Just like holding your breath triggers the stress response to fire, deciding to take deeper and longer breaths will send messages to your brain to slow down and relax. As you slow down and relax, you gain access to your higher brain centers and positive thinking capacity, which ultimately helps you regain control over your emotions and actions. This is why I call this time of breathing "power breaths." They are breaths that give you your power back and some semblance of control, even when distressed, as you will note in the next exercise.

Exercise 5.4: Refocusing on Tension While Breathing

When you are ready, think about the person or situation again. This time, however, maintain your power breaths, slowly counting to four as you breathe in and counting to five as you breathe out. Ask yourself the same questions:

- What do I want to do to this person or situation?
- Do I feel like there is a solution?
- Do I feel in or out of control of the situation?
- If I were to pick up the phone and call this person or even run into him or her right now, how would I react?

Write down your thoughts and observations.

_____

_____

_____

_____

_____

_____

_____

If you practice this breath cycle for ten to twenty minutes, you will achieve greater peace of mind. If you were to practice this meditation for ten to twenty minutes every day, your entire body and mind would start becoming more resistant to stress, allowing you to maintain your calm more often and a stronger sense control over your emotions and reactions. Using your breath or other forms of meditation techniques helps you transcend your negativity, quiet the mind chatter, shift into a more positive physiological response, and ultimately respond better, even under duress.

The key is quieting that inner negative voice—the one that is holding onto stories from your past of being a victim; the one who feels out of control and invisible; the one who keeps forgetting that you are actually strong, valuable, and loved.

How to Make the Shift

You have already practiced a breath exercise that helps quiet the mind and relax the body. For the most part, meditation can be that simple. The first step is to make a choice to redirect your focus away from your negative thinking to something else—your breath, a word, phrase, prayer, sound, object, or movement. By concentrating on a particular focus without judgment, repeatedly, over a period of time, the chatter in your mind can dissipate, enabling the stress response to relax, along with the muscles in your body. There are many techniques available to you to practice with, but I find that using a breath focus, progressive muscle relaxation, or guided imagery is the easiest to start with.

Progressive Muscle Relaxation

A very effective way to reduce tension is actually by creating tension first, believe it or not. The technique of progressive muscle relaxation (PMR) involves first tensing a particular muscle group, like the forehead or neck, for several seconds and then allowing those same muscles to relax for about thirty seconds after, noticing how your muscles feel as you relax. You can start with the muscle groups on the top of the head and move to the soles of the feet or start from your feet and move to your head.

PMR is a wonderful way to reduce stress and anxiety, especially if you practice it often. It helps you become more familiar with what the various muscles of your body feel like tense versus relaxed. As you develop a keener sense of awareness, you can then cue this relaxed state to happen the moment you start feeling tense. I also like to think that the tensing and relaxing of your muscles is mirroring the process of being stressed and letting go. This means the more you practice, the easier it will be for you to let go of your tension and therefore your stress.

Exercise 5.5: Practicing PMR

To practice PMR, I recommend finding a quiet place to sit, where you can be comfortable without falling asleep. Though this is a great exercise to do when you are in bed and unable to fall asleep, your goal is really to be able to stay relaxed, not asleep, despite being tense, so that you can use this technique during times of stress.

When you are ready, close your eyes and do five power breaths. Then . . .

- Focus on your **right foot** and tense/squeeze only the muscle related to the right foot (curling your toes under) as tight as you can so that it is uncomfortable to you but not painful for about five seconds.
- Now let all those muscles relax as all the tension flows out of the muscles into the earth. Notice the tension leaving the muscles of your right foot as you take two, three, or more power breaths (it should take about fifteen to thirty seconds).
- Move on to your **right lower leg and foot**, squeezing the calf muscles as tight as you can by bringing the toes toward you for about five seconds.
- Relax the muscles of your right lower leg and foot, noticing the tension releasing and flowing into the earth, as you take two, three, or more power breaths.
- Move on to your **entire right leg**, squeezing the thigh muscles, the calf, and the toes as tight as you can for about five seconds.
- Relax the muscles of your entire right leg, noticing the tension releasing and flowing into the earth, as you take two, three, or more power breaths.
- Do the exact same process with your **left foot**, **lower left leg**, and **entire left leg**.
- Move on to your **right hand**, squeezing the muscles as you make a fist as tight as you can for about five seconds.
- Relax the muscles of your hand, noticing the tension releasing and flowing into the earth, as you take two, three, or more power breaths.

- Move on to your **entire right arm**, squeezing the muscles as tight as you can as you tighten your biceps by drawing your forearm up toward your shoulder and making a muscle while clenching your fist for about five seconds.
- Relax the muscles of your entire right arm, noticing the tension releasing and flowing into the earth, as you take two, three, or more power breaths.
- Do the exact same process with your **left hand** and **entire left arm**.
- Move on to your **buttocks**, squeezing the muscles of your buttocks as tight as you can for about five seconds.
- Relax the muscles of your buttocks, noticing the tension releasing and flowing into the earth, as you take two, three, or more power breaths.
- Move on to your **abdomen**, squeezing the muscles of your abdomen by sucking in your stomach as tight as you can for about five seconds.
- Relax the muscles of your abdomen, noticing the tension releasing and flowing into the earth, as you take two, three, or more power breaths.
- Move on to your **chest**, squeezing the muscles of your chest by taking in a deep breath and holding it for about five seconds.
- Relax the muscles of your chest, noticing the tension releasing and flowing into the earth, as you take two, three, or more power breaths.
- Move on to your **neck and shoulders**, squeezing the muscles of your neck and shoulders by raising your shoulders up to your ears and holding them there as tight as you can for about five seconds.
- Relax the muscles of your neck and shoulders, noticing the tension releasing and flowing into the earth, as you take two, three, or more power breaths.
- Move on to your **mouth**, squeezing the muscles of your mouth by smiling as big as you can, tensing your jaw muscles as tight as you can for about five seconds.
- Relax the muscles of your mouth, noticing the tension releasing and flowing into the earth, as you take two, three, or more power breaths.

- Move on to your **eyes**, squeezing the muscles of your eyes by squeezing your eyes shut as tight as you can for about five seconds.
- Relax the muscles of your eyes, noticing the tension releasing and flowing into the earth, as you take two, three, or more power breaths.
- Move on to your **forehead**, squeezing the muscles of your forehead by raising your eyebrows high as you can for about five seconds.
- Relax the muscles of your forehead, noticing the tension releasing and flowing into the earth, as you take two, three, or more power breaths.

If you take fifteen minutes to practice PMR on a regular basis, it counts as your meditation practice for the day, which means your overall stress levels will be reduced. As I mentioned, the more you practice, the better you get to know your body and how the muscles tense or relax in different states. Then when you feel stressed, you can cue your muscles to relax, which will have the effect of dissolving your stress.

Guided Imagery

Another extremely effective form of meditation for managing stress involves guided imagery, where you use your imagination to picture a place, person, or time that makes you feel peaceful, relaxed, and happy. The goal of this type of practice is to help you cultivate the ability to be relaxed and at ease through the engagement of all of your senses as well as your imagination. When you imagine, for example, being on a white sandy beach, feeling the sun shining down on your skin as you inhale the refreshing sea air into your lungs, your thoughts shift away from everyday chatter and your body relaxes. The more senses you engage while imagining such a positive experience, the more your mind will believe you are actually there, taking you further away from your negative emotions, thoughts, and stress.

You can use your imagination to picture a beautiful and happy scene or to work through negative emotions such as anger through the use of mental images. For instance, you can visualize your anger as a symbol or object and imagine it dissolving into dust. I often use golden light that shines down from the sun above (or heavens) that dissolves hurts into dust and fills up my heart, mind, and body with love and peace instead.

Like PMR, the more you regularly practice guided imagery, especially for ten minutes or more, the better able you are to cue yourself with the same imagery to create relaxation and peace during stressful times. It is best to practice in a quiet setting, where you are comfortable and not easily disturbed. Put your phone away and put a DO NOT DISTURB sign on your door if you have to. You may choose your office, bedroom, parked car, bathtub, or create a meditation area in your home. The more you rehearse when you are not stressed, the easier it will be to use this imagery when you are in a bad mood or triggered.

Exercise 5.6: Happy Place Visualization

- Close your eyes.
- Take note of how you feel. You may rate your negative emotional intensity at the time from zero to ten (ten being very upset, angry, sad, and so forth, and zero being you feel no negative emotions). Take note of how your body feels as well.
- Do five or six power breaths, deciding to let go of your emotions and thoughts every time you exhale.
- Bring your thoughts and imagination to something positive. For example, imagine yourself in your favorite place in nature—perhaps relaxing on a beach, walking through a forest, hiking on a mountain, lying in a hammock, working in your garden, watching the sunset from a boat—or in a place where you are always happy and relaxed.
- Take note of all the details: What are you feeling? How are you feeling? What are you wearing? Who are you with? How does the air feel on your skin? What colors do you notice—the blueness of the water, colors of the sky in a sunrise, the rosy cheeks of someone you love? What sounds do you hear—waves crashing against the shore, birds singing, or leaves moving in the breeze? Do you taste or smell anything—salt on your lips,

chocolate or the aroma of wood burning in a fireplace? The more details you can find and the more senses you evoke, the better, as this memory engages your concentration in a direction that is opposite to your negative thinking and anger.

- Wherever you find yourself, imagine yourself feeling happy and at peace and smiling. Try to stay with this imagery, exploring all of your senses for at least five to ten minutes.
- Take note of how you feel now, rating your negative emotional intensity from zero to ten.
- If you feel sufficiently relaxed and when you are ready, do another five or six power breaths.
- Remind yourself that you can go to this wonderful place any time. It is yours to go to.
- Now open your eyes.

As I mentioned, when you quiet the mind, relax the body and breathe deeply for an extended period of time, you meditate. When you add in visual imagery intended to not only create calm but also address the stress and underlying negative beliefs, you can heal on a deeper level as well. You can use imagery to explore your negative emotions and where they originate from and to imagine new situations that dissolve the negative feelings. In addition, when you combine peaceful and loving visual imagery with physical exercises, like PMR, you can train your mind and body to associate certain peaceful images with the relaxation of the muscles. Again, the more you practice this technique, the more your body learns how to be cued to let go and relax.

Exercise 5.7: A Meditation Combo

Whether you choose to do this meditation in the moment for a few minutes when you are upset or as part of your meditation practice, you will benefit, as it combines PMR with imagery in a way that can help you dissolve your stress and find bliss.

- Close your eyes.
- Take note of how you feel and rate your negative emotional intensity level.
- Do five or six power breaths.
- Imagine the sun is shining down upon you, golden rays of healing light full of love and wisdom.
- Tense your forehead, squeezing the muscles of your forehead by raising your eyebrows as high as you can, then hold your breath for about five seconds.
- Exhale slowly as you imagine the golden light shining down on the top of your head and now moving down your forehead, causing the muscles of your forehead to relax and release all the tension.
- Tense your mouth, squeezing the jaw muscles, smiling as wide as you can, then hold your breath for about five seconds.
- Exhale slowly as you imagine the golden light shining down through the muscles of your face as they relax and release all the tension.
- Tense your neck and shoulders, squeezing the shoulder up to your ears, then hold your breath for about five seconds.
- Exhale slowly as you imagine the golden light shining down through the muscles of your neck and shoulders as they relax and release all the tension.
- Tense your chest and abdomen, squeezing the muscles of your abdomen and holding your breath for about five seconds.
- Exhale slowly as you imagine the golden light shining down through the muscles of your chest and abdomen as they relax and release all the tension.
- Tense your buttocks, squeezing the buttocks muscles, and hold your breath for about five seconds.
- Exhale slowly as you imagine the golden light shining down through the muscles of your buttocks as they relax and release all the tension.
- Tense both your arms and hands, making fists as you flex your muscles, then hold your breath for about five seconds.

- Exhale slowly as you imagine the golden light shining down through the muscles of both your arms and hands as they relax and release all the tension.
- Tense both your legs and feet, squeezing your thighs and curling your toes under, and hold your breath for about five seconds.
- Exhale slowly as you imagine the golden light shining down through the muscles of both your legs and feet as they relax and release all the tension.
- You are filled with and surrounded by golden light.
- Take another five or more power breaths.
- Take note of how you feel.

Keep in mind there is no right way to meditate. There is only the right way for you that gets you relaxed and feeling at peace. The more you practice, the better you get. Do not judge yourself or worry if your mind chatters while you are trying to focus. Simply notice that your mind is active, imagine your thoughts floating away, and bring your mind back to your focus. Practice, practice, practice. Try yoga, tai chi, transcendental meditation, Buddhist meditation, and so forth. You never know, you could become your own Zen master someday! Tune in to the next chapter where you will learn more about mindfulness meditation.

Chapter 6
Mindfulness to Calm Your Madness

....

"Mindfulness is about love and loving life. When you cultivate this love, it gives you clarity and compassion for life, and your actions happen in accordance with that."

—Jon Kabat-Zinn

As long as you look outside of yourself to be happy, you will invariably find yourself being unhappy because you will always feel like an empty well needing to be filled. The emptier you feel, the easier you will be to trigger, resulting in negative behaviors, actions, and thoughts, causing you to feel worse. The key to your happiness does not lie outside of yourself, therefore, but within.

Thus far, I have been guiding you to become aware of how you feel, your body's sensations, and the intensity of your emotions and thoughts. When you are able to witness such observations of yourself without judgment—understanding that there exists no right or wrong and that you are simply witnessing you, as if you are watching a movie of you—you will be able transcend the emotions, the past, and the stress to find you can exist in the present moment, which is full of bliss. Nothing is good or bad, right or wrong. Such witnessing has its roots in the Buddhist meditation practice called mindfulness, a widespread secular practice today, that involves being in a moment-by-moment awareness of your thoughts, sensations, and feelings, as well as of the surrounding environment. Open observation or witnessing ultimately allows for better recognition of pervasive underlying beliefs and emotions as well as patterns that are creating an imbalance.

The practice of mindfulness has many benefits—physical, psychological, and social. Studies have shown that the practice of mindfulness meditation invigorates the immune system, improves positive emotions, reduces the effects of stress, and alleviates depression.[15] Mindfulness has been shown to help tune out distraction and improve memory and focus.[16] Jon Kabat-Zinn created the mindfulness-based stress reduction (MBSR) program at the University of Massachusetts Medical School, a model now used globally, including in schools, prisons, and hospitals.[17] In short, practicing mindfulness can improve your physical, psychological, and mental health and is a perfect technique to use to manage anger so that it doesn't manage you.

Exercise 6.1: Mindfulness versus Anger

Let's take a scenario and play it out in two different ways. Mark down how true or how false each scenario may be as it applies to you.

You've had a long day at work, and you are exhausted and hungry. You're getting home an hour late because there was an accident on the highway. You walk into your home and see that it's a mess. No one in your family has bothered to do their chores. You can feel your anger starting to boil up and you . . .

    A. Break down and start screaming at your family to clean up their mess. You ream into your spouse for not having your back and supporting you with the care and discipline of the children and home. You go to your room, slam the door, and throw yourself on the bed.

Very True   **Very False**

             1   2   3   4   5   6   7   8   9   10

B. Take a deep breath and begin to observe the emotion rising in your body, your heart rate speeding up, as well as your breathing rate. You notice your jaw is clenched, as are your fists. You notice that your face feels red. You take another deep breath. And then another and then another, for ten full breaths, all the while observing the sensations in your body as well as your thoughts. You continue taking slow deep breaths, and as you exhale, you release the thoughts and the physical sensations out with your breath. Watch them float away. You let go. Now, you communicate.

Very True   **Very False**

1   2   3   4   5   6   7   8   9   10

Though it may seem that the latter example takes a lot of effort, the reality is that it takes more effort to explode. It is more probable that you will feel spent and exhausted after a bout of rage than after an opportunity to breathe and let go. The magic words here are "let go." When you let go, the anger no longer has a hold on you. When you let go, you become unattached to your situation, your emotions, and your negative stories, and the result is that you feel lighter and freer.

Un-Attaching without Judgment

Any time you get stressed, or rather, distressed, you become caught up in a story of negativity. You hold on to that story tightly, like a dog with a bone, unable to let go.

When practicing mindfulness, you calmly accept everything—feelings, thoughts, beliefs, sensations, and situations—without judgment, even if negative. You allow yourself to be in the now, the present moment, simply witnessing everything, as if you are watching a movie without being attached to the outcome. You are not attached to what happened yesterday or what will happen next. You are not attached to anything because you are curious about what is happening in the present moment. And when you do so, when you allow yourself to be in the present moment, nonjudgmentally, you free your emotions from taking hold of you.

Normally, you think about what you should have or could have done or what you can do or not do. Your emotions take you back to a past that is over and often no longer relevant, and your anxieties or assumptions cause you to jump forward to worrying about a future that has yet to happen. Every time you like or dislike, love or hate something, someone, or some situation, you judge. Every time you judge, you get trapped in the past or in expectations of the future because your judgment is based on how the world or circumstances have made or will make you feel. And with this judgment comes a heightened negative emotion. With a heightened negative emotion comes the stress response. Even the simple use of a negatively charged word can stimulate the stress response, negative emotions, and corresponding negative beliefs and actions.

Exercise 6.2: Awareness of Sensations That Occur with Words

Take note of the sensations and feelings or emotions that rise up for you when you repeat these statements to yourself. Using adjectives or sentences, best describe your experience.

A.   I hate it when people are late.

_____

_____

_____

B.   I don't like waiting in lines.

_____

_____

_____

C. I enjoy being curious, and I observe how I feel when I am waiting for people.

_____

_____

_____

_____

D. The breeze feels cool on my skin as I wait here in line.

_____

_____

_____

_____

As you can see, A and B elicit negative emotional responses, whereas C and D do not. You most likely observed your stress response activating in your body with the mere thought of having to wait in line. Did you feel the anxiety or frustration rise through your body when you stated A or B? Did you notice feeling differently when stating either C or D? These latter cases involve you observing the situation with openness while being in the present moment. There is no attachment and no entrapment in judgmental thinking. The situation isn't different, but how you choose to observe or engage in the situation is.

Un-Attaching versus Detaching

It is important to note that you are un-attaching, not necessarily detaching. When you shift your focus into the present moment, you loosen your grip on giving your thoughts and emotions so much power over you and how you see or define yourself in the world. When you focus, you do so with non-judgment and love, essentially letting yourself be in the world as you are, without feeling bad about you or anyone else.

In contrast, detaching involves distancing yourself or creating a wall that separates you from something or someone without necessarily changing bad feelings, ultimately creating a big gap of separation that prevents you from experiencing true joy and bliss, communicating well, and forging intimate relationships. Un-attaching entails observing your emotions or thoughts without giving them any power, as if you were observing the colors in the sky, the aroma of flowers, or the sound coming from the birds singing in the trees. With un-attachment, you are not separate from anything or anyone, but rather, part of a larger whole.

Mindfulness meditation will help you feel un-attached, calmer, and caught up with the drama in your head or your life. Your relationships can improve, as can your physical and psychological health. The first step is to make the decision that you want to be free of these attachments.

Setting Yourself Free

If you start paying attention, you will notice that you are pretty attached to your thoughts and old stories. If and when something happens to you that upsets you, how many times and to how many people do you repeat the story? How fixated do you become on the story, the person, or the situation? How long does it take for you to let go?

By deciding to focus on the present moment, you choose to disengage from your old habits of thinking that really do not serve you. The more you un-attach from these old paradigms and instead focus on being in the now—on your thoughts or emotions as they come and go, in a state where you are completely true to yourself and your true nature—the more peaceful and liberated you become. With practice, you can get to the point that you are able to live your life mindfully all of the time. The first step: practicing letting go.

Exercise 6.3: A Simple Practice of Letting Go

- Close your eyes.
- Do three or four power breaths. Just focus on the breath as it moves into your lungs, fills them, and then flows out of your lungs so they deflate.
- Open your eyes.
- Look around you. Notice the objects around you. What are you noticing that you didn't notice before? Or did you know everything was there when you first closed your eyes? Gaze and observe everything around you.
- Close your eyes again.
- Go back to focusing on breathing, but do not do power breaths. Just breathe regularly. Sit quietly without trying to judge, change, or make anything happen. No need to do anything at all but sit quietly and let yourself simply be aware. If thoughts come through, be aware of them, but do not focus on them. Same with feelings, ideas, or stories. Notice them popping into your mind without focusing on them, allowing yourself to simply be aware of anything and everything. You may notice sounds around you, a breeze on your skin, or how your body feels where it is sitting. You are not focusing on any of it, just noticing. You are allowing yourself to rest in this silence, being present and aware. Observe and relax for as long as you can.

How did that exercise feel for you? Write about your experience.

_____

_____

_____

_____

_____

_____

_____

_____

Many people find it challenging to shut down thoughts or stories when meditating and trying to be silent. In this exercise, you are not meant to be trying to do anything, least of all shutting anything down. Instead, you are accepting the thoughts, feelings, or emotions as they occur and watching them come and go.

I do recommend sitting in silence like this for at least five minutes a day, perhaps prior to starting your day and at the end of your day. The longer, the better, as the more you practice this simple mindfulness technique, the more at peace you will become in general, meaning that the level, frequency, and duration of distress you experience daily will diminish. The best part about mindfulness is that you can do it anywhere and in any situation. You can take a mindful shower—noticing the smells of the soap, the feeling of the water, or the sound of the water as it drops down. You can eat mindfully—appreciating the smells, tastes, and sensations. You can be in life mindfully, especially when you are stressed, using your skills to un-attach and find your calm.

Using a Mindful PAWS

If you haven't figured it all already, all the tools I have given you thus far incorporate some aspect of mindfulness, whether it is using the four-step process to assess your distress of validating, witnessing, labeling, and noticing; using the TMI as you assess your triggers, mood, and infrastructure; or having a meditation practice. Mindfulness is the glue that aligns everything you have learned so far together, and I have created a pneumonic that will help you apply it with ease. It's called PAWS.

Pause: When you find yourself getting stressed, your first step is to pause and take a breath or two to begin the process of removing yourself from the emotion and the drama.

Acknowledge: Once you have paused, then take a moment to acknowledge and validate that a strong emotion is present. You notice the emotion without getting caught up in it.

Witness: The next step is to take some time to witness what and how you are feeling.

Separate: As you witness your thoughts and feelings, the next step is to imagine you are watching a movie play out to help you separate yourself from the experience, choosing not to identify with the emotion, the situation, or the pattern of thinking that you have noticed you were engaging in.

Exercise 6.4: Applying PAWS

Here is an opportunity to apply PAWS to a situation. Perhaps something happened today that upset you, or something causes you to get riled up with anger, anxiety, or distress when you think about it. Think about that situation now and take note of how upset you get simply by thinking about it. Now . . .

Pause

- Do five to ten power breaths, counting to three as you breathe in and counting to five as you breathe out.

Acknowledge

- Acknowledge that anger, anxiety, or distress is present and honor its presence, understanding that it is there for a reason right now, usually to signal that you are out of balance and not in tune with yourself, your truth, and your value.
- Validate the way you are feeling instead of denying or repressing it.
- Let the emotion be there and take advantage of this opportunity to breathe deeply and breathe in loving kindness and honor to yourself.

Witness

- Observe and take note of the sensations that are occurring in your body, where the sensations are happening, and what they are like.
- Notice what thoughts, phrases, or stories are running through your head, observing if you are using phrases like, "It's not fair," "Why me?", or "I can't take this," or if there is a pattern to your thoughts that you recognize and can label.
- Observe if there is tension or relaxation of any muscles or body parts, discerning where the emotion itself seems to be located, as well as its intensity, shape, form, and effect on your breath or posture.

Separate

- As you observe your body, your emotions, and your experience, choose to see your negative emotion and your expression of this negative emotion as a pattern, a story that is playing out like a movie.
- Observe the story knowing that it doesn't define you.
- To help yourself separate from the experience, also gently observe your breath as it moves in and out, the sounds in the room that come and go, the birds singing in the trees, the lawn mower humming outside, or the sounds of cars driving by.
- Witness everything around you.

After applying PAWS, you may feel less charged and less stressed. When you create space between you and your emotions, you liberate yourself from needing to be identified by the external worlds, old stories, or beliefs. When these stories and the negativity no longer have a hold on you, you find more peace and calm. Mindfulness, therefore, enables you to be more objective as you validate and label any given situation—your reaction, your trigger, where your infrastructure is lacking—without your emotions clouding your insight.

For instance, let's assume that you have done the exercises in the previous chapter and identified several categories or labels for given situations that bring about the same feeling or negative belief. Once you have your categories, you can easily recognize the associated feelings when they arise and therefore objectify them. You might say something like "This is what I experience when I feel invisible," or "When I feel that some sort of injustice is happening, my heart clenches shut and I have a hard time breathing," or "The movie of injustice is a pattern of heart clenching and difficulty breathing associated with thoughts of things being unfair." Taking the time to label an experience once or twice allows you to identify a pattern quickly in the future so that you can observe it as it is happening, not get swept away with it. You essentially separate yourself from any given situation or drama so that it loses its power over you. The more separation you create, the better capable you are of shifting your stress reaction to a loving or calm response.

Shifting Into Appreciation

When you allow yourself to be in the present moment, un-attached, nonjudgmental, and open, you can make the choice to shift into a state of appreciation. If you think about it, stress is a state of "not enough." When you are worried that you do not have or are not enough yourself, it is rare that you can also be in a state of appreciation. By shifting intentionally into appreciation, you invariably shift your mindset away from not being enough to feeling lucky.

The good news is can choose to appreciate anything you wish. You can appreciate the moon, the stars, the way your breath moves, the sounds of laughter, that there was a yesterday and that there will be a tomorrow somewhere, that you get to have a today, that you get to experience all the emotions you are having, that you are living and breathing, that someone gave you life, and so forth. As you shift into appreciation and gratitude, you shift into the lucky state of love.

I recommend that you build a daily practice of appreciation into your life so that it becomes a common state of being for you. You can sit quietly for five or more minutes every day and hopefully every evening to contemplate things you appreciate, perhaps even writing them down in an appreciation journal. Try it out for yourself in the next exercise.

Exercise 6.5: The Appreciation Contemplation

- Bring your awareness to your breath. Follow your breath as it moves in, and follow your breath as it moves out.
- Be aware that your breath connects you to all of life.
- Be aware that you can't hold on to your breath even if you try.
- Be aware that when you breathe, you breathe in all of the air; you don't get to select which air you breathe.
- Be aware that your life is similar as you get to have a myriad of experiences, not just select ones.
- Be aware that you get to breathe and you get to have a myriad of experiences.
- Be aware that you get to see the moon, you get to see the stars, and you get to see the sunrise the next morning.
- Appreciate. Appreciate the moon. Appreciate smiles. Appreciate dogs. Appreciate sidewalks. Appreciate apples. Appreciate friends. Appreciate people who come into your life to wake you up. Appreciate all that you have and are. Appreciate anything that comes to mind.
- Appreciate for as long as you need to.

Exercise 6.6: The Appreciation Journal

When you are done with your appreciation meditation, jot down a few things that you are truly grateful for in a journal, especially with regard to positive experiences or realizations you have had during the day or week. It can be something minor, like feeling lucky that you found a parking spot, to something major, like falling in love or getting the job you wanted. I usually recommend writing in your journal in the evening and then reading what you wrote to yourself the next morning and contemplate further how lucky you feel for having had these experiences prior to starting your morning meditation. Example starting statements for your appreciation journal can include:

I am so grateful that _____

I am lucky because _____

I am so appreciative of _____

Chapter 7
Redirect Stress for Good

·······················

"Raise your words, not your voice. It is rain that grows flowers, not thunder."

—Rumi

L ike a gust of wind, stress can be a powerful force that can instigate radial change, new direction, standing up for justice and civil rights, and protecting those you hold dear. It motivates strangers to band together to pick one another up from under fallen rubble or fight together for a common cause, fuel political agendas, promote business transactions, end or align relationships, or enable people to feel more in control of something they normally fear. But like the winds that arise from a tornado, the effects of stress, especially when associated with anger, can be destructive if not kept under control. So too, if the powerful force of stress or anger is bottled up inside of you and not expressed or moved, the energy will combust internally or explode externally, like a soda can that is shaken and eventually opened. The key is to learn how to move stress with structure and direction so that its effects can benefit you and others rather than destroy.

Learning from Our Ancestors

Wisdom traditions like traditional Chinese medicine (TCM), Buddhist philosophy, and the Vedic system have alluded to the positive benefits of transforming negative emotions to their more viable and healthy forms for thousands of years. In the Five Element System of TCM, anger, one of the more destructive negative emotions, is perceived as a negative energy form that is associated with an imbalanced liver, stagnation, explosive growth that causes roots to fall out of the earth, and a variety of health problems like anxiety, high blood pressure, blood clots, and liver disease. When counterbalanced positively, the energy takes on associations with loving kindness and compassion, strength, creativity, swiftness of action and movement, gentle growth, the sound "shhhh," the color green, and the season of spring.[18]

In the Vedic tradition, which dates back to 2000 BCE in India, the chakra system also provides a guide for the shifting of anger into a more positive form. Chakras, which mean "wheels" or "whirls" in Sanskrit, are vortices of energy and consciousness that spin like the sun. There are seven major chakras in the body that are interconnected by the spinal column, each one associated with certain organs and physiological, physical, psychological, emotional, and spiritual functions, colors, sounds, and vibrations.

The chakra most affiliated with anger is the third chakra, located in the solar plexus. This chakra is located between the rib cage and navel and includes the upper abdomen, stomach, spleen, intestine, liver, pancreas, and gallbladder. It is believed that this energy center governs creative and intuitive abilities, as well as the rational side of the mind, assimilation of thoughts, the ego, and experiences that help you define yourself.

A healthy third chakra represents a healthy digestive system, whereby you know who you are, know what is nourishing for you and what is not, are able to absorb and assimilate life's experiences in a healthy way without losing yourself or being destroyed, and are able to let go and be rid of whatever it is that does not serve you, help you, or better you. An unhealthy third chakra is represented by feelings of insecurity, self-doubt and shame, the blame of others, anger, anxiety, and a myriad of digestive problems.[19] The key for balance involves connecting to the earth, meditating, breathing, getting centered, and loving kindness for the Self and others.

What does this mumbo-jumbo mean?

You now know that it is possible to manage negative emotions by controlling the stress response, which you can do through developing awareness and being mindful, employing breathing techniques, developing a meditation practice, connecting with love, and keeping your infrastructure intact. Ancient wisdom traditions support the use of these tools to not only control the stress response but to transform the negative stress energy into loving energy that benefits you and others. The bottom line is that these traditions give you more tools to not only reduce your stress but redirect the energy to one that you can do good with. These tools involve getting the stressful energy to loosen up and not hold you captive so that you can get grounded and centered in your power, and ultimately, shift into love.

Move It to Loosen It

When you pay attention to how your body feels when you are stressed, you will notice a feeling of constriction or restriction in your musculature or within your body somewhere, as if your energy is blocked or stagnant. What do you do when energy is blocked? You move it. The best way to move this energy is by moving yourself, whether it is aerobic exercise or meditations in motion as done in yoga, tai chi, qigong, or progressive muscle relaxation. This energy can also be "moved" through the use of music, verbal sounds, or bodywork like massage and acupuncture.

Physical Activity

Aside from being good for your physical and mental health in the long term, exercise, or physical activity, has the added benefit of helping you burn off excess energy and release endorphins and other feel-good chemicals that improve your mood, even when you are in distress. When stressed, consider jogging, walking, bicycling, swimming, or jumping rope. You can rollerblade or dance or play basketball, tennis, or football. Weight training is also a good option. Whatever you choose to do, be careful, as you could be so caught up in your negative thoughts, you may not pay attention to your form and hurt yourself. I personally find physical activity to be a wonderful release from my anger and frustration. I also find slower movement practices like the gentle martial art forms of tai chi or qigong, or even yoga, help move negative energy while also helping create a sense of calm and peace. I call this meditation in motion.

Exercise 7.1: Shake It Out

- Let yourself think about something frustrating or upsetting. Allow the stress to rise up and pay attention to where the body and your breath feel constricted or restricted.
- Allow your arms and hands to drop to your sides.
- Begin to wiggle your legs, followed by your buttocks, followed by your torso.
- Add the arms and shake them wildly, while also shaking your head.
- Shake your entire body for one minute, as if you are shaking all the stress out.
- Notice how you feel.

Meditation In Motion

When you don't have the option to get to a gym or go outdoors to exercise, you always have the ability to do stretching and relaxation exercises wherever you are. Progressive muscle relaxation, for example, is a highly effective technique that will certainly shift the stress-energy, as will a variety of breathing techniques and yoga poses. Particularly effective are poses that involve twisting at your core, which is meant to wring out the blocked energy in your third chakra. Below are a variety of exercises you can try. Choose one or do them all, one after the other.

Exercise 7.2: Supine Twist

- Lie on the floor (on a mat, a rug, or the grass) on your back.
- Bring your knees to your chest and hug them as you breathe in deeply, bringing them as close as you can to your chest.

- As you exhale, allow your knees to gently fall to the left side as your head falls to the right.
- Inhale deeply, and then as you exhale, pull your hips to the left with your left hand while your right arm stretches out to the right.
- Inhale, relax the tension, exhale, pull, and stretch.
- Do this for ten cycles of breath on each side.

Exercise 7.3: Kundalini Kriya Pose

- Sit on the floor cross-legged.
- Place your hands on your shoulders and wrap your fingers around your shoulders.
- Inhale deeply and twist to the left.
- Exhale completely and twist to the right, keeping your spine upright.
- Keep your eyes closed and twist twenty-six times.

Exercise 7.4: Alternate Nostril Breathing

- Take a deep breath in, then place your thumb on the side of your right nostril and press down as you exhale through your left nostril.
- Place your index finger on the side of your left nostril and press down, removing the pressure of the right nostril by lifting your thumb, and breathe in through the right nostril.
- Press your thumb back onto your right nostril while lifting your index finger from your left nostril and breathe out of the left nostril.
- Do this for twenty-six counts of breath.

Sound Therapy

According to the ancient traditions, a variety of sounds and chants can also shift the stress energy. You can vocalize these sounds or chants while doing your poses or while doing anything at all. The following exercises involve a few techniques that I use and find helpful.

Exercise 7.5: "Shhhh"

"Shhhh" is the sound that calms the liver, according to traditional Chinese medicine.

- Take one hand and make circular movements around your abdomen as if you are soothing your liver as you breathe in and then exhale with the sound "shhhh."
- Circle your hand around your abdomen clockwise nine times as you repeat "shhhh."
- Circle your hand around your abdomen counter-clockwise nine times as you repeat "shhhh."

Exercise 7.6: Shout "Ha!"

- While sitting or standing, taking a deep breath in and then shout "Ha!" as you exhale.
- Shout as loud as you can at least ten times.

Exercise 7.7: "Ha!" with Movement

- Stand with your feet shoulder-width apart.
- Raise your arms over your head and take a deep breath in. When you exhale, swing your arms down to your side aggressively, letting your head and body follow (so you flex at the neck and slightly at the hips) while shouting "Ha!"

Exercise 7.8: Sing Out Loud

- Find a song that you like and belt it out.

- Sing from the top of your lungs and from deep within your belly.
- Jump around and dance while you are at it.

Journaling Stress Out

Writing out your thoughts and feelings can be highly therapeutic, and I strongly advocate the use of a stress release journal, which involves writing down the reasons you are upset or stressed along with all your feelings without holding back or judging. This is the process I recommend:

Exercise 7.9: Stress Release Journal

- Set a timer for fifteen minutes or keep the time open.
- On a sheet of paper separate from your other journals, write down why you are upset or stressed and what you feel, see, think, or want to do.
- Don't hold back. Don't think too much. Write without filters. Get it out.
- You can draw pictures and use expletives or crude adjectives.
- Stop when the timer goes off or stop when you feel ready.
- Place your hands on the words you have written and say these words out loud: "I now release you from my body, mind, and consciousness."
- Destroy the papers by tearing them to shreds or burning them.
- Check in with yourself the next day. If you find that you are still upset or stressed a day later, do the exercise again.

Ground and Center Your Power

For most, it is quite challenging to sit still or quiet your mind when you are anxious or ruminating about something that you are upset about. Moving helps release this pent-up energy so that you can work toward being more centered, connected with yourself, and in control of your emotions and thoughts. One of the easiest ways to get grounded and centered is by spending time in nature. Here are four simple exercises to help you get there. The latter three exercises are especially helpful if you do not have access to nature.

Exercise 7.10: Centering in Nature

The aim of this exercise is to practice mindfulness meditation out in nature whereby you engage all your senses to appreciate everything around you while employing nonjudgmental awareness and appreciation to the connection you have with nature.

- Take yourself to a place in nature that you love. It may be a forest, an open field, a beach, or your garden.
- You may choose to stand still, sit comfortably, lie down, or assume the position of gardening, as long as you are comfortable.
- Take a moment to close your eyes.
- Notice the feel of the air on the skin of your face.
- Notice the feel of the air as it fills your nostrils and then your lungs.
- Notice the sounds of nature around you. Is there a bird singing? Are the leaves moving in the breeze?
- Notice the connection your breath brings to you with the air, the breeze, or the sounds.
- Notice the feel of the earth beneath your feet.
- If you are kneeling, notice the feel of the earth as you sweep it into your fingers and hands.
- Become aware of the earth, that it is what the farmers till and where your nurturance comes from.
- Appreciate the support the earth provides you.
- Appreciate that you are being nourished by the earth, the sun, the air, the rain, and anything else that comes to mind.
- Appreciate your place here on earth and your place in between heaven and earth.
- Breathe in and breathe out, deeply and slowly.
- You may choose now to garden mindfully, walk mindfully, or continue sitting or lying down using all your senses to appreciate your connection to heaven and earth—listening, noticing, looking, feeling, tasting, being.

Exercise 7.11: Rooting and Grounding

This exercise is a modified version of a qigong (a slow and ancient martial art form) movement that involves motion, balance, and using your imagination to ground yourself to the earth.

- Stand with your feet shoulder-width apart, keeping your knees slightly bent.
- Keep an upright posture with your head lifted, chin tucked, and back straight.
- Close your eyes.
- Do three to four power breaths.
- Bring your awareness to the soles of your feet and just be aware of the connection your feet have with the earth.
- Breathe in and imagine you are gathering the energy of the earth into the back part of the soles of your feet.
- Exhale, releasing the energy from the front pad of your feet back into the earth.
- Inhale, gathering the energy of the earth into the back part of the soles of your feet.
- Exhale, releasing the energy from the front pad of your feet back into the earth.
- Inhale, gathering the energy of the earth in the back part of the soles of your feet as you lean into the back of the soles, allowing the toes to come up slightly.
- Exhale, releasing the energy from the front pads of your feet back into the earth as you lean onto the front pads of your feet, allowing your heels to come up slightly. (You are swaying slightly back and forth with each inhale and exhale.)
- Imagine roots are being formed, moving deep into the earth, connecting you with the heart of the earth.
- Imagine the roots are giving you support and helping you stay balanced while allowing you to stay flexible and relaxed.

- Sway back and forth as you inhale and exhale, forming roots while staying flexible and relaxed, for at least ten cycles of breath.
- When ready, stand still. Be aware of your connection to the earth and notice how you feel.

Exercise 7.12: Child's Pose

This is a yoga pose that is very relaxing as well as nourishing. It helps you connect to the earth like a child might, letting go and breathing slowly in and out.

- Sit your buttocks on your heels on the floor (preferably on a mat, a rug, or on the grass where it is soft).
- Inhale deeply as you reach your arms upward.
- As you exhale, reach forward and lay your forehead on the floor.
- Stay in this pose for five minutes or more, just breathing.

Exercise 7.13: Liver Smile

This is one of my favorite centering exercises that involves doing an inner smile to your heart and your internal organs, particularly, in this version, your liver, while using the sound that is associated with balancing of the liver, "shhhh."

- Sit in a cross-legged position on a pillow or on a chair with your feet flat on the floor, whichever is most comfortable to you, and close your eyes.
- Do two or three breaths, breathing in counting to three and breathing out while counting to five, while noting the connection the base of your spine has with the center of the hearth and the top of your scalp has with the heart of the universe.
- Imagine the energy of the earth and the universe are connecting in your heart as you inhale and exhale.
- Smile gently.
- Smile as you gently move your focus and awareness to your heart. Smile in your heart. Acknowledge your heart as you smile, breathing in and out for another five cycles of breath.

- Continue to take nice, slow, deep breaths as you gently shift your focus and awareness to your liver, located under your right rib cage. Smile lovingly to your liver. Acknowledge your liver as you smile, breathing in and out for five cycles of breath.
- For the next five to ten cycles of breath, continue to smile inwardly and say "shhhh" every time you exhale.
- Sit quietly and notice how you feel.

Shift into Love

You have already learned about the importance of love and its healing powers on health and life, and hopefully you have experienced these benefits by doing some of the exercises and meditations. Since it is hard to access love when stressed, it is of course helpful to move the stress-energy first and then get centered. Once centered, you can transform the negative energy into something positive, using love to do so by assessing your TMI and seeing what you might need to do to improve your self-care or get more support.

Self-Care

Your TMI assessment might show you, for instance, that you are being triggered because you are sleep-deprived, lonely, hungry, or feeling irritable because you haven't exercised. As such, you first want to evaluate and actualize where you need to employ love with relationship to self-care. You can make a long-term plan (to sleep, meditate, eat better, and so forth) and a plan for the now. The "now plan" can include getting a massage or healing bodywork, treating yourself to a healthy meal, buying yourself flowers, or taking a needed nap. Whatever you choose to do, do so with loving-kindness toward yourself.

Social Support

Your TMI assessment will also show you if you need more support. You want to make sure that you have your "go-to" people who you can turn to in times of need. These are individuals you already identified or are working toward bringing into your life—individuals who can hear you, love you, or hold you without judging you. You would be surprised how many people you might know who can do this for you when you explain to them what you need from them. You can go to a support group, a therapist, counselor, or coach, or connect with dear friends or loved ones who can remind you how loved you are.

Help Someone Else

One of the most powerful ways to redirect and transform the energy of distress is by using the energy to do good rather than harm. Think about a cause that you can believe in and get involved with, and use your stress to motivate you to love and help this cause. If there isn't a particular cause that moves you, you can always help anyone who is in need. Get outside of your head and your emotions and look around you. Help an elderly person cross the street or carry their groceries home. Open doors for people and smile. Volunteer at a soup kitchen. The list is endless.

The Energy Socket

When in doubt and you are not sure what to do, who to help, or if you even feel like moving anymore, you can do this exercise that guides you to receive love and support from the resources around you, heaven and earth.

Exercise 7.14

- Sit in a cross-legged position on a pillow, on a comfortable chair with your feet flat on the floor or ground, or lie down on a soft blanket on the floor.
- Close your eyes and do three to four power breaths.
- Bring your awareness to the connection your feet, coccyx, or your entire back if you are lying down, have with the earth. Witness the connection and how the earth is supporting you—your weight, your livelihood, and

so forth. Allow yourself to imagine you are receiving nurture, abundance, and love as it rises from the heart of the earth through your body to your solar plexus.

- Bring your awareness to and focus gently on your solar plexus as you imagine you are gathering up the support, abundance, and nurture of Mother Earth into your solar plexus.
- As you inhale, gather the energy up your body into your solar plexus.
- As you exhale, imagine you are giving back love and generosity to the earth.
- As you inhale, gather more energy.
- Exhale, give back to the earth.
- Do this for five cycles of breath.
- Relax into your solar plexus, gently breathing in and out, noting the sensations you are experiencing, the expansion of your power, and the centering of your energy.
- When you are ready, imagine you are looking up at the sky and noticing golden rays of light shining down on you.
- As you inhale, imagine you are absorbing these golden lights that hold the support, nurture, abundance, and love of the universe.
- These light rays move down through the crown of your head and into your heart, filling your heart and spilling over into your solar plexus.
- As you exhale, imagine you are giving back love and generosity to the universe.
- Do this for five cycles of breath.
- Like an electric socket, you are receiving energy, support, nurture, abundance, and love from heaven and earth.
- Relax into your solar plexus, gently breathing in and out, noting the sensations you are experiencing, the expansion of your power, and the centering of your energy as you are now tapped into the heaven and earth.

Putting It All Together: What Redirecting Stress Might Look Like

Here is an example of what the process of changing the stress-energy to good might look like:

Your boss just took credit for the work you have been laboring hard over for the last two months. He barely even mentioned your work in his report to the CEO of the company. You are fuming. What do you do?

1. PAWS: Slow down your thoughts and just take a moment to pause. Acknowledge that you are angry and validate how you feel as you have every right to feel the way you do. Witness what you are feeling and the sensations you are experiencing and begin to label the experience (this is a situation of disrespect, dishonor, betrayal, etc.). Separate yourself from the emotion and circumstance as you label the experience and understand that you do not have to fall into the trap of the drama of anger.

2. Do your power breaths and feel yourself gently loosening yourself from your anger.

3. Move the anger energy by doing alternate nostril breathing followed by practicing the "Ha!" sound with movement a few times.

4. Once completed, do one the modified rooting and grounding qigong exercises.

5. Be still for a moment and contemplate and assess your TMI (trigger, mood, infrastructure).

6. Shift into love by practicing the energy socket. Make a list of activities you can do to help you feel seen, valued, and respected, understanding that being overlooked or disregarded is a pattern for you and that somehow you are co-creating the situation, which you will now work toward fixing.

7. Take note of how you feel.

Though this process does not change the outcome of what your boss has done, it will move you toward feeling less enraged and more empowered, ultimately helping you change the direction of your reaction and the course of action you might take in the moment and in the future. Any time you find an activity or action that allows you to shift out of a negative story, emotion, or reaction, write it down in your Distress Assessment Chart so that you know what you can do at a later date.

Distress Assessment Chart

What happened?	What is my physical reaction?	How is it making me feel?	How do I react?	What can I do to heal?	What is my new response?
Unsupported					
Ignored					
Rejection					
Humiliation					
Injustice					
Disappointment					
Grief/loss					
Illness/pain					

Chapter 8
Stand in Your Power

·······················

"When angry count to four; when very angry, swear."

—Mark Twain

There are some times when letting out a swear word or two can be extremely cathartic and sometimes empowering, especially when it is used as a mechanism to release the energy of stress and when it doesn't inflict harm on anyone.

Imagine this: You are late to work and stuck in traffic. Another driver cuts you off, causing you to step so hard on the brake that you spill coffee all over your new shirt. You lose it. Obscenities fly out of your mouth so foul you are almost surprised at yourself. A small part of you is even aware that the guy in the car next to you is staring at you and likely calling you a raving lunatic, which at this point, you are. But you feel a little better having gotten some of the anger out of your system before you get to the office.

The problem is that the day doesn't get much better. By the time you get to the office, a pile of papers a mile high is waiting in your inbox and your boss is demanding to have a file ready in the next ten minutes. You are stressed, overwhelmed, and wearing a stained shirt. When one of your children calls to tell you he forgot his lunch at home, you snap and lay into him, yelling at him for being irresponsible and lazy.

Ten minutes later, after giving said file to your boss, you find yourself sitting on the toilet, crying, angry at yourself for being angry, feeling ashamed and guilty for yelling at your child, and worried about losing your job if you don't get it together.

You need to get a grip. You try to remember what you read in this book, but you can't. You are too pissed off and burnt out. Your mind is blank, and you are just simply spent.

Sitting on the toilet with tears streaming down your face, you add it up: you are sleep deprived. Your husband didn't take out the trash, again. Your kids are constantly fighting, and it is a constant chore to get them to do their chores. Your boss thinks that it is okay to call you at night when technically your work hours are done at 5:30 p.m. Your mom can't stop reminding you how much better she was at being a mom, and you are beginning to think she is right. You can't remember the last time you got to the gym or got your kids to bed on time. All you want right now is a pint of ice cream and another shirt to wear that is not coffee-stained. You go through a list of shoulds—what you should have and should not have done over the course of the past week—and conclude that you are probably deserving of this big mess you are in. The further you go down this line of thinking, the more you cry. You swear, but it doesn't help. You feel like dirt and completely powerless. How can you get your power back?

Being Powerful

Many people think that being powerful means being aggressive, overbearing, dominating, or controlling. And because these qualities are viewed as negative, many people have contradicting feelings about what being powerful means. As a result, instead of standing in their power, many people, especially women, give their power away, not wanting to be seen as too aggressive or rude.

Standing in your power has nothing to do with how you treat people or whether you use force to get what you want. It refers to knowing who you are and standing by yourself and your beliefs. Power isn't something that comes from external measures but from an internal process of growth, love, acceptance, and awareness. In short, rarely does anyone take your power away; rather, you give it away.

Any time you believe you are not enough or do not have enough to manage adversity, you bring yourself closer to feeling powerless, whether it comes from incessant self-doubt and thoughts of being inadequate, feelings of being overwhelmed, worrying about what others may think, being upset that you are not being heard and have no voice, or feeling that you are not deserving of good or success. As long as you hold on to a "not enough" belief or thought, you sabotage your chances of standing in your own power. When you are not in your own power, you cannot fully honor yourself, what is important to you, who you truly are, what you truly want, what you are capable of accomplishing, or standing strong in your decisions. You are not solid in yourself, in your beliefs, or who you are.

Giving your power away happens the minute you take care of someone else's needs at your own expense. It happens when you do not say no and take on more than your plate can handle and when you let other people's feelings matter more than yours. It happens when you are not mindful of how tired, sad, hungry, or lonely you might be and when you criticize yourself by "should-ing" on yourself.

The "Should" Problem

I bet you have never paid attention to how many times you say "should" during the course of a day, either directing that "should" toward someone and what they should have done or toward yourself. You may not realize this, but every time you "should" yourself, you put yourself down and shame yourself. Statements such as "I should have known better," "I should have gotten a salad, not that burger," "I should lose weight" or "I should have gone left instead of right" underline the notion that you are not enough and need to be ashamed for this. When you berate yourself like this, the stress response gets triggered, and with that comes other negative emotions, memories of feeling similarly in the past, and the associated physiological changes.

Perhaps you can witness what should-ing yourself feels like and judge for yourself whether it gives a feeling of invincibility and expansiveness or smallness and contraction.

Exercise 8.1: The "Should" Test

- Close your eyes and say to yourself, "I should have _____." Fill in the blank with something you feel you should have done or should have been.
- Notice what happens to your chest and your breath.
- Do you feel contracted or expansive?
- Do you feel good or bad?

Comment here:

_____

_____

_____

Should-ing yourself doesn't inspire behavior change. Instead, it motivates maladaptive or negative coping behaviors that are self-sabotaging and effectively help you feel even worse than you did at the outset. In other words, saying "I should lose weight" will more likely provoke you to eat a tub of ice cream over a healthy salad, which will make you feel worse about yourself and more powerless to change. When you then feel bad about yourself and powerless, you are more likely to feel victimized by external circumstances, like a critical boss or a spouse who doesn't take out the garbage.

Exercise 8.2: The Alternative Statement

- Close your eyes and think about the same situation, but this time say to yourself, "I could have_____."

- Notice the sensations you experience in your body, particularly your chest and breath. Do you notice a difference?
- Does your chest contract in the same way if at all?
- Do you not feel more hopeful?

Comment here:

_____

_____

_____

By switching to "could," you have decided to be accountable for your behavior, knowing that doing things differently may lead to different results. You are not shaming yourself. You are acknowledging yourself without putting yourself down or dismissing yourself. Using "could" instead of "should" allows you to engage the stress response only enough to motivate action. "Could" includes a little bit of guilt to motivate thinking about behavior change but is not strong enough to induce inflammation, negative thinking, and the feelings of hopelessness and helplessness. Using "could" changes your internal conversations, quieting the inner critic so that you can be empowered versus disempowered, letting you be accountable for your choices and feel open to making some positive changes.

The "should" versus "could" exercise is a prime example of how your inner voice and negativity can sabotage your sense of Self and power. Using "could" more frequently gets you one step closer toward achieving the goal of feeling more empowered. The next steps entail quieting your inner critic that is having you "should" on yourself to begin with, assuming more powerful stances, aligning with your values and what you want, and changing your words altogether by aligning with your power statements.

Quieting the Inner Critic

We all have an inner critic. For some of you, that critic is a loud voice that tries to convince you that you are not enough through the framework of negative emotions, thoughts, and beliefs. When you are running on empty, when your infrastructure is down, or when you are under a lot of stress and overwhelmed, your inner critic gets louder and louder, cutting you no slack. It doesn't let you be human or make mistakes. It encourages you to sabotage yourself so that you continue not to take care or support yourself, and ultimately, it causes you to shame yourself and apologize for who you are.

The key is to quiet the inner critic and choose to accept and love yourself instead. Making this choice helps you embark on the path of taking care of you, which lets you heal from hurts, get healthy, get fit, understand yourself better along with your needs and wants, communicate your beliefs and desires with clarity and conviction, and stay unapologetic for what you believe and who you are.

Exercise 8.3: Quieting the Inner Critic

Let's say you find yourself depleted, tired, frustrated, angry, and disrespected. Let yourself go to this angry place right now.

- Allow negative feelings and thoughts to rise up. Take note if you feel powerless versus powerful.
- Pause and take a moment to acknowledge and validate that you are out of balance and that when you are out of balance, your inner critic comes for a visit.
- Rather than repressing the inner critic or the story that comes with your critic, or shaming or blaming yourself or anyone else for that matter, listen to your inner critic without getting caught up in it or believing it. What is it saying? You may wish to write it out here:

_____

_____

_____

_____

_____

_____

- Witness how the story is making you feel and causing your stress response to go into overdrive. You may wish to continue to write about the physical reactions you are experiencing here:

_____

_____

_____

_____

- Witness the negative beliefs this story is connected with, particularly related to how you feel about yourself and not having or being enough. Objectify the situation now by giving it a label and writing the associated findings down in your Distress Assessment Chart.

- Label: _____

- Look at what you have written with objectivity and appreciation that your inner critic is simply your warning signal that you are out of balance, triggered, and in need of love and care.
- In your chart, list activities or actions that you can do to love and take care of yourself.
- Take action by moving the negative energy. Whether you do physical exercise, meditation in motion, journaling, or sound therapy as discussed in the previous chapter, the result is the same: you move and destabilize the negative energy. If you are stuck in a bathroom stall at work and don't feel it is possible to move physically in public, then scream out loud, journal on toilet paper or your smartphone, or do one of the meditations in motion while sitting, like the Kundalini kriya pose or alternate nostril breathing.
- Center and ground. If you can get outside, take a mindful walk to help clear your mind and connect with nature. You can do the rooting and grounding exercise, child's pose, or liver smile.
- Choose to do an act of self-care, one that will help you feel empowered. Use this opportunity to fully evaluate your TMI and assess where in your life you may want to make changes that support you and your value more fully. This assessment will further your clarity and wants—from people, work, love, and in life.
- Note how you feel now. You may choose to write it down or simply contemplate your experience.

_____

_____

_____

The goal of quieting your inner critic is to help you believe in your worth. The worthier you believe you are, the less easily you will be overcome by stress or distress, and the more powerful you will feel and be. Of course, if you still feel stressed and lacking in power, you can always assume a power pose.

Redirecting the Energy and Power Posing

Amy Cuddy, a Harvard scientist who studies body language and the effect it has on hormones, conducted a study where subjects were divided into two groups. The first group was told to power pose for one hundred and twenty seconds before a mock job interview, while the second group was instructed to assume low power positions before their interview. The interviewers chose to employ the power posing group just about every time. When saliva samples were tested, those subjects who did the power poses had testosterone (which is a dominance hormone) levels increase by 20 percent, while their levels of cortisol (the stress hormone) dropped approximately 25 percent. The lower posing group had the opposite results, with increased cortisol levels and a drop in testosterone.[20] The best news is that this only take takes minutes! Here are a few exercises for you to try out.

Exercise 8.4: Stand like a Superhero

Stand with legs spread apart, arms on hips, and elbows bent. As opposed to the contracted state of feeling helpless, this pose opens up the body and conveys the sense of being powerful.

Exercise 8.5: Lean Back

Wherever you are sitting, lean back and lift your arms over your head, and cross them behind your head with your elbows out, leaning your head back on your arms (like a relaxing boss). Let your legs be shoulder-width apart and, if you like, cross one leg over the other, but only so that the ankle rests on the knee (not a full crossing of the legs). If you are at your desk, you can put your feet on the desk.

Exercise 8.6: Lean Forward

If you are standing near a desk or table, stand with feet shoulder-width apart, lean forward and place your hands on the table or desk and let them bear your weight.

The minute you decide to give your inner critic a new job, you choose not to be controlled by your negative beliefs and emotions and to take a stand for yourself instead, which you take to the next level by actually standing in a power pose. Assuming the power poses can then help you feel more self-assured. The more self-assured you are, the more clarity you gain regarding what you want and who and what you truly value, including what you value about yourself.

Getting Clarity about What You Want

Clarity is something you gain over time. For the most part, you often have to experience what you don't want in order to realize what you do want. The problem is that most people ruminate on what they don't want or don't like, rather than focusing on the opposite.

The more you hold on to a negative situation, the more you hold on to a negative belief or feeling, the more stress builds up in you—at some point, you explode. This happens when you think about a negative situation over and over again, tell the story repeatedly, or ruminate on it in any shape or form. The more you focus on how something or someone makes you feel negative, the more you deplete yourself, the worse you feel over time, and the less clear you become on what you want or deserve.

The key is to acknowledge and honor the way you feel, understanding that your feelings are appropriate and reasonable, but they are not helping you feel good or remedy the situation. Then decide to change those feelings to ones that are positive, are more powerful, and actually serve your well-being. Stating your thoughts and wants out loud repetitively will further enhance your feeling of power.

Exercise 8.7: Comparing Negative versus Positive Statements

You can experience for yourself the difference of how a negative versus a positive power statement makes you feel. Say these two statements out loud or silently to yourself and notice what happens to the physiology of your body and how you feel—contracted or relaxed, weak or strong, powerless or powerful.

1. I am tired of being disrespected.
2. I embody the feeling of being respected.

Describe the difference:

_____

_____

_____

By repeating statements that are more powerful and positive, you override the negative thoughts, emotions, beliefs, and especially physiology. The more powerful you begin to feel, the higher chance you will think and act with clarity and calm going forward.

Creating a power statement is fairly simple, especially once you have identified your label in your Distress Assessment Chart since you just choose the opposite belief or feeling from that label. You can also create a separate Power Chart to analyze more specifically not only the power statement that best suits your needs but also what role you are playing in preventing yourself from feeling powerful.

Exercise 8.8: Creating Power Statements

Create five columns with the following headings: "negative feeling," "my role in it," "preferred feeling," "power to change," and "power statement."

Power Chart

Negative feeling (label)	My role in it	Preferred feeling	Power to change	Power statement

Step 1. Negative feeling: Begin by looking at the column in your Distress Assessment Chart that contains words that describe how situations make you feel with regard to the state of not being enough. Write those words down in the first column of the Power Chart, labeled "negative feeling."

Step 2. My role in it: Think about what role you had in co-creating this feeling. Ask yourself: In what way do I also cause myself to have this feeling? Do I disrespect myself? How do I disrespect myself? Do I betray myself? etc.

Step 3. Preferred feeling: Think about the opposite of the negative feeling and what you really want to feel. If you feel disrespected, then choose respected; seen or heard to replace invisible or ignored; valued to replace devalued, and so forth.

Step 4. Power to change: This is where your previous TMI assessment comes in handy and other exercises you have done thus far that guide you to action steps that support you positively and are in your power to change. What can you do to support yourself to feel better and be healthier and more empowered? What are alternate behaviors you can employ that are healthier and more loving toward yourself? Fill out this column based on your TMI assessment.

Step 5. Power statement: Once you have figured out what your preferred feeling and what may be in your power to change, create a power statement out of it.

Example Power Chart

Negative feeling	My role in it	Preferred feeling	Power to change	Power statement
Disrespected	I don't respect myself by not eating healthy and putting myself down.	Respected	I can respect myself by eating healthy and loving myself.	I choose to feel respected and release all feelings of being disrespected.
Unimportant	I don't make myself a priority when I don't say no to people.	Important	I can make myself a priority and say no when appropriate.	I choose to be a priority and release all feelings of not being important.
Unsupported	I don't support myself by not getting enough sleep and not taking time out for myself even for short periods.	Supported	I can support myself by taking little breaks to breathe, meditate, walk, or rest.	I choose to feel supported and release all feelings of not being supported.

Exercise 8.9: Putting It All Together

Once you fill in the chart, you will have a list of power statements available for you in times of need. The process that brings everything together that you have learned thus far might look something like this:

Example: You are sitting on the toilet crying and fuming. You feel powerless, disrespected, and angry.

Step 1: PAWS

Pause with power breaths, acknowledge, witness, and separate. Breathe in, count 1-2-3. Breathe out, count 1-2-3-4-5. Do this for at least four cycles of breath, while acknowledging and witnessing the sensations in your body and what you are feeling.

On the fifth cycle, breathe in, count 1-2-3. Breathe out, count 1-2-3-4-5, and ask yourself, "What or how is this making me feel with regard to not being enough (i.e., disrespected, invisible, devalued)?" Observe without judgment the feeling that comes forward.

Continue your power breaths as you come up with the feeling.

Step 2: Label and assess TMI

If you haven't already created a label for your Distress Assessment Chart, do so now and write it down. Take a close look at the reasons you may have been triggered (old memory of hurt, lack of sleep, feeling sick, etc.)

Step 3: Move the energy and get centered

Continue to breathe, do one of the movement exercises, or go for a nature walk.

Step 4: Let go and release

Resume power breaths, and during the fifth out breath, say to yourself, "I release this feeling of feeling_____ (i.e., disrespected, invisible, devalued) as I have no use for this feeling." As you do so, imagine that you are releasing the feeling or the energy of the feeling into the clouds, the earth, the ocean, or anywhere else you want to send it.

Continue your power breaths and repeating this statement for at least five cycles of breath.

Step 5: State your power statement

As you continue your power breaths, switch over to repeating
your power statement: "I choose to feel _____
(i.e., respected, supported, or loved), so I align with this feeling
of feeling _____ and embody the feeling
of_____ now and in the future. In fact, I really enjoy
this feeling of _____ and choose to stay feeling
_____."

Repeat the Step 5 power statements at least five or six times,
then take note of how you feel. This is also a good time to assume a
power pose.

This practice may not make you feel completely better, especially not right away
(though it can), but it will start creating change within you so that you are less
likely to be pushed overboard in subsequent negative situations. You may need to
repeat the statements for a whole day and sometimes longer. The more you do it,
however, the more you reprogram yourself to shift away from the negative story
and move into your story of success and empowerment permanently.

Chapter 9
Laugh and Let Go

....

"Laughter is the tonic, the relief, the surcease for pain."

—Charlie Chaplin

Imagine this: You are in your power. You feel confident and open to what life has in store for you. You are in the present moment, and as you look at your life and at yourself, you realize it is really one movie, and you get to choose whether it is a dramatic tragedy or a romantic comedy. You also get to choose whether you wait your entire life for a happy ending or decide to have a continuous happy journey, understanding that if you wait for a happy ending, for that something perfect that doesn't exist, nothing will ever be enough and you will be perpetually disappointed and depleted and yes, stressed.

I remember coming to this realization long ago when I met a colleague for a business lunch at a nearby restaurant. As we had our meeting, I became a little distracted because a little boy, perhaps three years of age, started making funny faces—not at me or anyone in particular, but just experimenting with the muscles of his face and entertaining himself. His mom, who appeared to be having a serious conversation with another adult, intermittently chided him for not eating his food and to get his face off of his cup (he often mushed it against his mouth). He then proceeded to not listen to his mom, jumped off his chair, and laid down on the floor. Every time his face touched the cool ceramic floor, he would giggle.

It made me giggle too.

His mother, as most adults would be, was annoyed, worried that he would pick up terrible germs, and angry that he was not behaving as he was taught. Kudos to her that she did not yell or raise her voice, having instead scolded him quietly and placed him back in his chair. He didn't cry, but he was quite disappointed. His pancakes were not as interesting as the floor, but the ice in his drink was!

Would I have done the same thing if I were the mother in this situation? I wondered. Probably. I would have been annoyed with my child for disturbing people, including me, and if I were sleep-deprived, upset about something, worried, or anxious, the chances that I would be angry with my child are quite high.

I realized that if I were to truly practice being in the present moment, with a childlike state of awe and curiosity, I would probably want to lie down and put my face on the floor too, to feel the coldness of the tile and see what it was like. I would probably giggle like a three-year-old, given the chance. It sure would have made my serious meeting more palatable, not to mention that the giggling would certainly have eased my tense muscles and probably have gone a long way in helping me manage my stress.

Why Laughter Eases Stress

If you think about it, laughter is highly social and part of the human way of life that allows us to bond and get through difficult times. When you laugh, it is rare that others don't laugh with you, as it is usually contagious. When people laugh together, their guards are brought down, self-control gets thrown out the window, and a sense of togetherness occurs. When you feel bonded and united with others, your sense of belonging and having social support improves. Having this support improves well-being and the ability to handle adversity, strengthens your infrastructure, and lowers stress.

Humor and especially laughter are great forms of stress relief. Laughter, for instance, stimulates physical changes in the body, including the increase of circulating endorphins, or happy, feel-good chemicals. Like progressive muscle relaxation, laughter induces an increase of the stress response and muscle tension, followed by relaxation and a reduced heart rate, respiratory rate, and blood pressure. Though studies are inconclusive, laughter may improve your immune system, mood and oxygen consumption, and relieve pain. Laughter is a good no-side-effect intervention for managing stress.[21]

As human beings, we naturally bring humor into hard situations to help us temper the pain of a memory. Think about a situation that happened to you in the past that was extremely difficult at the time but now you retell as a funny story. How long did it take you to be able to do that with that particular memory? Are there some memories you simply cannot find any humor in?

The deeper the wound, the more hurt you hold on to, and the more likely this memory will serve as a trigger to your distress. When you bring humor into the equation, you change the lens of how you view the memory. You lighten it up a bit, which offers you a more open perspective that enables you to see the situation more objectively. In short, humor and laughter help you let go of your attachment to the negative memories and beliefs, turn down your stress response, connect to a happier mood and therefore happier memories, and ultimately, manage painful or stressful situations better.

Exercise 9.1: Appraising with Humor

Step 1: Bring your thoughts back to a time when you felt humiliated, humbled, or embarrassed by someone else's actions. Let yourself feel the pain of the experience, without reliving it. Simply observe the body's physical response and the emotions that come forward, as you have learned to do.

- Do you feel contracted or expansive?
- How would you label what you are feeling?
- What about the situation was humiliating?
- How did it make you feel about yourself?
- How did and/or do you feel about the person or persons that enabled this situation to happen?

- Write out your thoughts, answers, and observations.

Step 2: Implement PAWS.

- Inhale deeply and exhale completely.
- Observe the breath as it moves in and out.
- Observe the chest as it rises and falls.
- Witness the way you are feeling while also observing the breath as it moves in and out.
- Separate yourself from the experience as you practice mindful awareness of the present moment.

Step 3: Allow yourself to take a step back so that you can look at the experience as if you are watching a comedy movie with main characters and supporting actors.

- Observe the movie and notice which of the scenes are quite funny, or could be.
- Will it be a slapstick comedy, with someone tripping or falling?

- Perhaps it will be a Woody Allen–like movie, where the comedy comes with words and subtle nuances?
- Write out the new story.

_____

_____

_____

_____

_____

_____

Studies have shown that humor is an optimal strategy to cope with negative situations, especially when reappraising later memories, as it helps people feel better when confronted with negative stimuli without skewing or minimizing the memory itself.[22] Being able to look at your life with humor, therefore, enables you to honor the memory, your feelings, and the situation, while also giving you the chance to see the bigger perspective without contracting into your smaller Self and falling into a negative thinking and behaving pattern. The more often you are able to find humor in your life, the better you will be at reappraising with humor on a regular basis.

Lightening Up and Being Unapologetic

For me, laughter and humor reflect more than just improved coping styles or the ability to socialize better. They are also my segues to lightening up and becoming more childlike, open, curious, and amused by life, rather than threatened by it.

Children don't apologize for being themselves. They simply are. They are not tormented by the past or by expectations of a future that is yet to happen. They don't care yet what others think. Children, by virtue of being curious creatures, want to explore, learn, touch, feel, giggle, or snort. Most adults, on the other hand, have lost their childlike sense of play and curiosity and are usually riddled with fear based on past experiences or being judged, or worry regarding expectations of the future. Adults do possess, however, a fully functioning mind and the ability to discern, learn, or grow from past experiences, enabling them to make wise choices regarding the future.

The key is to combine one's childlike sense of play with the wisdom of having lived without falling prey to fear and negativity. I call it lightening up.

Lightening up means not taking yourself and situations so seriously and being light of heart, open in mind, and unapologetic for who you are.

We were all brought up to meet the expectations of others and told to behave in a certain way that inevitably was done at the expense of our spirit and natural personality. Most of us have been following the rules and meeting the expectations of others for so long, we find ourselves wondering who we truly are, often having trouble making decisions, and feeling selfish if we want something different or insecure if we do not fit the perfect mold.

Stepping into your power means you get to be unapologetic for being you while also getting to laugh at you.

You can be unapologetic for being rambunctious, having messy hair, being someone who manages to spill things or trip everywhere she goes, being smart and a bit funny, getting mad or hurt sometimes, and being gentle and kind. You can be unapologetic for being you and laugh at your imperfections.

The more you stand in your power, the more you can accept yourself for who you are—your humanness, your strengths, and your weaknesses. You can get closer to this state by bringing laughter and humor into your life. The more you are in your power, the more you will laugh and be able to connect to your childlike state of being.

Moving the Negative Energy with Laughter

There are many options available to you to work on your funny bone and to bring more humor into your life, including when you are angry. In fact, laughter—especially in the form of laughter yoga, comical posing, and joke journaling—is a great way to move stress energy. I do find that it is not always easy to employ laughter techniques during times of distress, but it does get easier to do so, especially if you have done the work to heal yourself and your memories, as described in the previous chapters.

Laughter Yoga

Laughter yoga, also known as Hasyayoga, is a yoga practice that involves gentle breathing, stretching, and voluntary laughter. Started in 1995 by Dr. Madan Kataria, who believed that laughter could provide many benefits physically and otherwise, laughter yoga was meant to be done in a group setting, whereby eye contact and group laughter eventually led to genuine contagious laughter. I don't mean little giggles here and there. I mean the big belly laughter that makes your eyes water and your stomach ache. You know, the one that is catching and usually makes everyone around you laugh too.

The key here is that the laughter is done with others, not at others, for at least ten to fifteen minutes. The laugh is a deep and loud laugh, coming from deep within, so it is a virtual release of pent-up energy. You can imagine how cathartic this might be. You might imagine that by the time you are really belly laughing, all cares and worries are thrown out the window, allowing you to be more childlike and playful.

Given that when you are stressed you may not have the ability to jump into a class for laughter yoga, it is possible to practice on your own, which I do recommend. Why? Because the more you practice laughing, the better you will be at commanding your body to laugh when needed (like commanding your muscles to relax when practicing progressive muscle relaxation), and the more relaxed and playful you will become overall. The more relaxed and playful you feel, the greater the chance that you will feel unapologetic. The practice normally involves first clapping, then breathing, then laughing.[23]

Exercise 9.2: Solo Laughter Yoga

Step 1: Warm-up

- Rhythmically clap your hands together, making sure there is full contact of all parts of the palm of the hand and fingers.
- While doing so, chant "Ho, ho, ha, ha, ha!" repeatedly, at least three times. Clapping of the hands together is believed to stimulate acupressure points and get energy moving around, while the chant activates the diaphragm and gets the body to breathe more deeply.
- You can move your hands up and down, or swing them from side to side, continuing to clap rhythmically with the sounds

Step 2: Power breaths

- To ensure that you breathe in and out from deep within the belly, you can do a few power breaths, raising your arms up and smiling as you breathe in, and letting your arms fall back down and relaxing as you breathe out.

Step 3: Activate laughter—the laughter gradient

- Begin by smiling.
- Slowly start to chuckle.
- Allow the chuckle to build up so that you start laughing. Laugh harder and louder until you peak with loud belly laughter.
- Feel free to flail about and slap your knees.
- Slowly bring that laughter down to a chuckle.
- Quiet down the chuckle until you are smiling again.

Step 4: **Centering and grounding the laughter**

- Do your power breaths and laugh if and when you feel like it for two to three minutes.
- When you are ready, sit quietly with your power breaths, allowing your body to come into a calm and grounded state, for as long as you need to.

Comical Posing

In the previous chapter, you practiced holding poses that would enable you to feel more powerful. You can hold these poses with a twist of comedy to bring a lightness to your mood and situation without causing you to feel worse, ashamed, or less than.

Exercise 9.3: Superman/Superwoman with a Twist

If or when you are feeling the anger rise up, do the following:

- Assume the superman/superwoman pose.
- Put on a cape or imagine you are actually wearing a cape.
- Walk around as if your muscles are swollen and big, with your hands on your hips and legs outstretched as you walk (no bend at the knees).
- Talk out loud about how you will use your superpowers to vanquish the rascals.

Exercise 9.4: Curse Like a Foreigner

- Stand with your legs spread shoulder-width apart.
- Hold one arm up with elbow bent and finger pointed to the sky.
- Curse with a foreign accent or a pirate's accent.

Joke Journaling

When you find yourself upset about something, especially when you note that you are likely overreacting, sit down and write about the situation as if it were a slapstick or romantic comedy, or if you can, write three or four jokes. For example, you can go back to the scenario when you came home to a dirty house with screaming children. You can write about a scene where you tripped over something and then managed to do a somersault in the air, while simultaneously grabbing a dust cloth and single-handedly cleaning the room before landing perfectly on your feet. This is your chance to be creative. Give yourself at least five minutes to write, and don't think too hard about it. Have fun with the process.

Exercise 9.5: Comedic Writing

- Write out a few details describing what happened to make you angry.
- Write the words down from the story on another sheet of paper, but this time, keep large gaps or spaces between the words.
- Insert sentences, curse words, or anything else you like, including pictures, in between the words to create a comedic story.

Centering and Grounding with Joy and Laughter

Practicing laughter yoga is a great start to getting grounded, especially when you allow yourself to embody the feeling fully. In addition, you can play in nature or use your imagination.

Exercise 9.6: Mindful Play in Nature

- Find a place in nature where you can feel safe to relax and let go.
- Practice mindfulness, but do so as if you were a curious child seeing things for the first time.
- Pick up branches with a sense of lightness and curiosity.

- Lie down on the ground and feel the earth beneath you.
- Smell the flowers, skip, and inhale the breeze into your lungs.

If you do not want to go outside or are in a situation where you can't leave or show outward expression of being a child, you can visualize while sitting quietly instead. Doing this exercise will certainly put a smile on your face and make people wonder what you are up to!

Exercise 9.7: Visualize

- Start by imagining yourself as a child.
- See yourself running around, laughing hysterically, simply not caring about anything but how funny something is.
- Imagine that you are skipping, hopping, giggling, and snorting—all in your imagination of course.
- Let your imagination run wild and have a good time!

The minute you implement humor or laughter, you start the process of redirecting your stress in a more positive direction so that you are better able to observe a situation for how it has made you feel, label it, and create and activate a power statement that best suits you. Assume a power pose and then walk around like a top model or superhero and then curse in a foreign language, which will certainly enable you to feel more powerful yet lighthearted.

You can also use your good humor to redirect conflicts or disagreements and to ease tension and tempers. Keep in mind that if you try to use humor when you are really distressed, you may end up making snide remarks that are hurtful and insensitive, as you are simply trying to cover up your emotions with humor rather than redirect them. For this reason, you want to move the energy and get centered first. When centered and grounded, you are more able to use humor and playfulness to open up pathways of communication and compassion.

Maintenance of Your Funny Bone

In order to tap into your sense of humor, especially during difficult times, it is a good idea to work on honing and maintaining your funny bone on a regular basis. If you use it, you won't lose it. More than this, any measure you can take to engage your funny bone and to help you keep a positive mental attitude will benefit not only your mood but also your health and your relationships. Think about it: the lighter you are, the less seriously you take yourself, and the less upset you will be when life doesn't go as planned.

Here are some activities you can partake in regularly to strengthen your sense of humor:

1. **Look for humor in all the right places.**
   Make an effort, at least once a week, to watch a funny movie or TV show. You may choose to read the comics, go to a comedy club, read a funny book, or go to a yoga laughter class.

2. **Smile as often as you can, for no reason.**
   If you look around you, you might notice that most people are caught up in their thoughts and rarely smile. Take it upon yourself to smile for no reason. You might find the world starts smiling with you. And if they don't, they will wonder what you are up to.

3. **Schedule playtime.**
   At least once a week and if possible, once a day, schedule some time to play. You can do anything that feeds your creative side. You may wish to draw, paint, sculpt, do jigsaw puzzles, or do some sort of sports activity for fun. Whatever you choose to do, aim for at least twenty minutes, which will give your brain a break and help you feel more relaxed and refreshed after.

4. **Spend time with people who make you laugh and happy.**
   The more you surround yourself with people who make you laugh and happy, the more likely you will be reminded that your life is pretty darn

good and that you have a lot to be thankful for, especially funny and lively friends. Remember, laughter is contagious.

5. **Keep a gratitude journal.**

   One sure fire way to be on the road to angry is to feel sorry for yourself and unlucky. The luckier you feel, the less likely you will blow up when life doesn't go your way. Take a few minutes daily to write down three or four reasons you feel grateful. Make a list in which you are counting your blessings.

6. **Spend time with children.**

   As adults, we forget how to be playful and how to see the world with an open heart. Spend time with children and observe them. Try to be silly with them or simply have a chat with them.

7. **Laugh with yourself.**

   Laugh with yourself as often as you can, seeing the lighter side of your ways, without putting yourself down. The less seriously you take yourself, the less easily you will be triggered.

8. **Strike a pose.**

   Have a daily practice in front of your mirror of striking your superhero comic pose. Walk around your house with your finger in the air and speak with a foreign accent when you are telling your family the plans for the day.

Chapter 10
Get to Compassion and Forgiveness

....

"When you look deeply into your anger, you will see that the person you call your enemy is also suffering. As soon as you see that, the capacity for accepting and having compassion for them is there."

—Thich Nhat Hanh

You are pissed off, and you want to get even. You want to see the person who hurt you suffer. They deserve it. It would feel good to see justice playing out.

True? Would you get satisfaction from seeing the offender suffer? Would it ease your tension and anger?

The truth is that if you do experience any elation after getting revenge, it is not usually long-lasting. In the end, when your actions come from a place of anger, fear, and hatred, the result is never good. What sort of action would stem from this negative place anyway? Would it be something that would align you with feeling good about yourself as a person? Indeed, research suggests that getting revenge doesn't offer much happiness. Rather, it appears that people who exact vengeance are angrier after completing the act of revenge compared to those individuals who did not have a chance to.[24]

For example, college students were challenged with playing an investment game with the following potential two outcomes: everyone cooperates, everyone benefits equally. One person refuses to invest, that person benefits at the expense of the group. Within each group, there was a secret experimenter, called the free rider, who convinced the group members to invest equally but actually did not go along with the plan when the time came to put up the money. These free riders gained more than twice the money that the rest of the group received. Some of the groups were also offered some ways to get revenge on the free rider by spending their earnings to punish this person. Whoever was given the option to get revenge, did. In other words, no one opted out. Participants then completed the survey, which showed that all groups believed they would feel better if they had the opportunity for revenge, even the group that was happiest at the start. Interestingly, the group that did get revenge felt worse after the act than those who had not had the chance to.[24]

The significance of this study is in its triviality. Imagine if the situation were direr when your emotions are highly charged and your actions spiteful. The likelihood is that you would not feel good about yourself because you had been betrayed and because you acted unkindly. It would be a lose-lose situation.

Though revenge may offer temporary satisfaction, in the end, it hurts you more. Similar to drinking alcohol, taking drugs, or partaking in any other type of addictive behavior, acting out with revenge stems from a very low place in your search to feel better, which means the act will only help for a minute and eventually lead to feeling worse. In this case, you are also hurting someone else, which may negatively affect your psyche more than you realize.

Why might you want revenge? Because you are angry that someone dared to take your power away and devalue you, and you want to regain your power, especially over the wrongdoer. Food for thought, though—if you never lost your power to begin with, would you still want revenge?

The truth is, you can choose to give your power away and act out with revenge, or stand in your power and act from your highest Self for the highest good. It's your choice.

The Wolf You Feed

An old Cherokee legend tells a story of an old grandfather who speaks to his grandson about why there is violence and cruelty in the world. He says to his grandson, "In each human heart, there are two wolves battling one another. One is fearful and angry, and the other is understanding and kind." The grandson then asks, "Which one will win?" His grandfather answers, "Whichever one we choose to feed."

Which wolf within you will you feed, and what are you going to feed it? Will you feed the wolf of anger and revenge or the wolf of love and compassion?

Exercise 10.1: Connecting with Compassion

Step 1: Think about a time when you felt wonderful, perhaps a time when you fell in love or had a great success at work or play. Imagine that time right now.

- Notice how even the mere thought of such a time allows your heart to open and a smile to form on your face.
- Take note of how your body feels. Is it tense or relaxed? Is your heart open or closed? Your mind tense or at ease?
- Take note of how much is bothering you when you allow yourself to stay focused on this wonderful time.
- Imagine now that you are extending compassion from your heart to the world.
- Notice how this feels in your body.
- Write down your experience.

_____

_____

_____

_____

_____

_____

Step 2: Now think of the opposite scenario—a time when you felt tired, overwhelmed, unhappy about the way you looked, or dissatisfied with your life or an outcome of something important to you.

- Take note of the sensations you experience in your body.
- Does your heart feel open or closed? Does your body feel tense or relaxed? Does your mood change overall? Does your chest expand or contract? Is your mood positive or negative?
- Try to send compassion from your heart out to the world.
- Note the experience and write it down.

_____

_____

_____

_____

_____

This exercise is meant to guide you to observe the two expressions of yourself: your higher Self and your lower Self, superhero versus victim, loving and compassionate versus fearful and angry, and so on. Making the choice not to feed the victim within you and instead to feed the loving superhero (or peaceful warrior) is your challenge.

You can't be blamed for wanting revenge when angry, especially when you have been wounded and when you are triggered. But is that the wolf you want to feed? What if you chose to understand that all human beings suffer, and it is from this suffering that we hurt others. Would you want to be a part of the cycle that continues this suffering, or end it by choosing to forgive?

Compassion and Forgiveness

It isn't easy to forgive, just as it is challenging to let go of hurts, and it can take years and years for pain to diminish, let alone disappear. It is of course this pain that causes you to feel distressed and react with anger or revenge. This very same pain can guide you to uncovering and healing old wounds so that you can truly stand in your own power and strength of character and live your true potential filled with love, joy, and success. It is from this place that forgiveness is possible.

Understand that forgiveness is not about condoning poor behavior but rather offering a gift of compassion for the person who has wronged you because you know they suffer while also offering compassion toward yourself because of your suffering.

When you manage to get to a place of forgiveness, you succeed in deciding that you want to live from your highest Self and potential, rather than lowest, knowing that despite your pain, you will grow, learn, and love. The key is to remember that this place of power, love, and centering is within you and never leaves you, even in the hardest of times.

As Thich Nhat Hanh wrote in his book *Anger* in reference to compassion and forgiveness, "When it is raining, we think that there is no sunshine. But if we fly high in an airplane and go through the clouds, we rediscover the sunshine again. We see that the sunshine is always there. In a time of anger or despair, our love is still there also. Our capacity to communicate, to forgive, to be compassionate is still there. You have to believe this. We are more than our anger, we are more than our suffering. We must recognize that we do have within us the capacity to love, to understand, to be compassionate."[25]

Compassion and Forgiveness Always Start with You

You cannot force yourself or "try" to be compassionate, centered, or otherwise. If you are stressed, overwhelmed, sleep-deprived, and not functioning from your bliss, the attempt to be compassionate is just that—an attempt. The effort to be compassionate is of course better than an effort to be vengeful, but the result will not be one of helping you, not the other person, feel better in the end, but will rather result in resentment on your part and more negative behavior on the other person's part. I'm sure you can think of a situation in your current life with a friend, colleague, spouse, or family member where you tried to be compassionate and it backfired.

If you are trying, you are not being.

Period.

You either are compassionate or you are not. You are either being present and mindful or not. You are either at peace or not. And if you are not, you cultivate it. This means you take care of yourself first. Take a PAWS. Pause and become mindful of the way you feel, of your thoughts, feelings, emotions, and the interaction that you are taking part of. Step back and witness. Breathe in and out. Observe and do not judge. Give yourself some breathing space. When you create the breathing space, you create an opportunity for change, growth, and compassion to come in, along with the hearing, listening, speaking, and understanding that is not influenced by negative judgment, emotions, or beliefs. You create space for the healing of your heart so that you can have space in your heart for another person and their suffering.

The practice can go something like this:

Exercise 10.2: Breathing in Space for Compassion

1. Slow down your thoughts and just take a moment to PAWS. Take three to five power breaths.

2. Acknowledge that you are angry and validate how you are feeling. You have every right to feel the way you do.

3. Witness what you are feeling and the sensations that you are experiencing. Begin to label the experience (this is a situation of disrespect, dishonor, etc.).

4. Separate yourself from the emotion and circumstance as you label the experience and understand that you do not have to fall into the trap of drama and anger. Do your power breaths.

5. When you are ready, breathe in compassion and love into your heart center. When you exhale, let go of everything else—your thoughts, emotions, confusion, memories, and so forth. Breathe in love and compassion, and let go of everything else that is in your mind, body, and especially heart. Do this for another five to ten power breaths.

6. Connect to beauty. If you are outside, look up at the sky, smell the flowers, listen to the raindrops, or feel the breeze on your skin. If you are inside, use your imagination to remember a time in nature, appreciating the experience using all your senses.

7. Connect with the love and compassion within your heart with the beauty of nature and your feelings of appreciation and gratitude.

8. Observe how you feel now, and if you wish, write about it.

_____

_____

_____

_____

_____

_____

_____

_____

_____

Did you notice how much lighter you felt by the end, more open and loving? In this state, you are more capable of being truly compassionate and understanding. Without nourishing yourself, especially your heart, you cannot have the full capacity to be forgiving or compassionate for another.

For this reason, the process of compassion and forgiveness always starts with you. You take care of you first and then re-evaluate how you feel. It may take a long time to get to a place where you can be forgiving or even open to it, but that is okay. The more you heal yourself, the better you will be in life in the long run, which is why sometimes, compassion for yourself may come in the form of doing a little re-parenting.

Re-Parenting You

If you were to recognize that within you is still a little boy or girl who feels unloved and not good enough, you might be more mindful of being good to yourself and upholding loving and self-care behaviors on a regular basis. Realize that the more you do not take care of yourself, the more you ignore this little child. The more unloved and ignored this little child feels, the more often you will be triggered in getting angry in challenging situations.

It, therefore, may benefit you to re-parent yourself.

What does it mean to re-parent? It simply means you make sure you go to bed early, take your vitamins, eat healthy, think good thoughts, take time to play, have play-dates, and so on. It also means that sometimes, when you PAWS, you use your imagination to do a little cuddling with a younger version of yourself, an especially effective method to use when you are feeling distraught, overwrought, and angry, as it is a very definitive way of showing yourself compassion. Soothing your own heart enables you to stay more open and capable of understanding someone else and the pain they may be experiencing.

Exercise 10.3: Re-Parenting Visualization

1. Once you PAWS, close your eyes and breathe love and compassion into your heart center as you did in the previous exercise.
2. Imagine that as you breathe in and out, your heart gently begins to open.
3. Envision a younger version of yourself.
4. See yourself enveloping this younger version of yourself in your arms.
5. Hold him or her close and then look into his or her eyes and say these words, "I see you. I hear you. I understand you. I love you." Repeat the same sequence of words another three or four times, holding the younger version of you close to your open heart.
6. Note how you feel, particularly the state of your heart and level of emotional intensity.
7. Write down your observations if you wish.

_____

_____

_____

_____

_____

_____

_____

_____

_____

_____

_____

_____

_____

_____

Combining this soothing visualization with the compassion and gratitude practice will set you faster on the path to feeling at peace and being able to more easily let go and forgive because your heart will be more open. To open your heart even more, you can also get back in touch with the rambunctious, playful, and joyful side of you.

Dancing Babies

Do you remember the dancing baby that first appeared in the 1990s? (I'm sorry if this example pre-dates you.) I remember it from an old TV show called *Ally McBeal*, where the main character, Ally, would frequently have hallucinations of seeing a baby dancing (of course in the most inopportune and stressful situations). It was back then that I realized this visualization was quite a useful tool for me and my patients, since it brought a smile to the face and reminded one of being more carefree and silly.

I personally used this imagery several years ago when sitting in a very stressful meeting with a board of directors. As the tension in the room escalated, I found myself feeling angry and upset, very close to storming out of the room, raising my voice, or both. I knew that neither action would be wise, so instead, I imagined myself as a little girl, dancing around without a care in the world. As the arguing continued around me, my little girl-self twirled and waved her arms in the air, causing me to smile and become increasingly less attached to what was transpiring in the room. When it was my turn to speak, my voice remained calm and my words were objective and rational. The best part was that everyone intently listened to me, and I didn't care whether they did or not.

Now it is your turn to try it out.

Exercise 10.4: Kid-ing Around

1. Once you PAWS, close your eyes and breathe love and compassion into your heart center as you did in the previous exercise.
2. Imagine that as you breathe in and out, your heart gently begins to open.
3. Envision a younger version of yourself, perhaps yourself as a toddler or a young child.
4. Imagine this child dancing, laughing, twirling, skipping, jumping, or doing any other activity you can think of that will make you smile or laugh within. The sillier and more carefree the movement, the better.

5. Imagine you can hear your favorite song in the background and you are now joining this little version of you, shaking your booty, giggling, or twirling.

6. Note how you feel.

The goal of kid-ing is to enable you to feel lighter and less attached, and closer to your innate ability to be joyful and full of appreciation. The more un-attached and joyful you are, the more connected you can be with the part of you that can forgive and live with compassion.

Getting to Forgiveness

Forgiveness is an end-goal that you can hope for and work toward. It is the ultimate experience of freedom, of not caring, and of being free of stress. Know that you are never under any obligation to forgive, as it is not easy to get there. True forgiveness, like true compassion, comes from a place of love and fullness, of being able to understand and accept that all humans suffer and that it is because of this suffering that we can forgive. True forgiveness is not about letting people off the hook for mean or hurtful actions, denying or repressing your own feelings, overlooking anything or anyone, justifying bad behavior, being contingent on religious paradigms, or being the better person. Rather, it is about being free from suffering, distress, fear, hate, anger, resentment, and old negative stories that have kept you bound and unhappy. Your heart is open, full of love and compassion for your own plight and for the plight of others.

Forgiveness is not a single act that you do once in a lifetime. Rather, it is a process that takes time, often a lot of time, to understand and work through your own distress, heal yourself, and find compassion within yourself first before you can expand your good will outward. Forgiveness, in other words, is a state you get to when you are ready to rewrite your story of success rather than continue to live in your story of suffering. Forgiveness is letting go of the negativity for good.

Know that from a health perspective, forgiveness is associated with many improvements, from self-esteem to reduced anxiety and depression, decreased blood pressure, less substance abuse, a greater sense of well-being and fulfillment, and overall better physical health.[26]

So how do you get there?

Some of you may be finding that after doing the practices in this book, you are already in a place that is more forgiving, a place where you are ready to let go. Whether you are in this place or not, there is always more you can do to truly be able to forgive and be in a place of bliss and peace.

The Steps to Get You There

1. PAWS it.

Keep in mind that without you acknowledging your own pain and taking care of yourself, achieving true bliss, as opposed to drug-induced or numbing types of bliss, will be near impossible. For this reason, the first step is always going to be PAWS, where you stop and acknowledge your feelings, enable yourself to observe and be in the present moment and remove yourself from the emotional intertwining of the situation you find yourself in.

If you are having thoughts of revenge, for example, take a pause. Acknowledge and honor that you are hurt and that there is reason you want revenge. Take a moment to notice how your body is responding to the thoughts. Notice if thoughts of revenge cause your heart to open or to close. Notice if the thoughts cause you to truly feel light, happy, and joyful, or more negative.

2. Take care of you.

Make a choice to keep your heart open. Do the breath exercise, breathing in love and compassion. Choose to take care of you right now. You may want to do the re-parenting practice followed by the kid-ing exercise as well.

3. Understand that we all suffer.

When you feel your heart is more open, remind yourself that all human beings suffer to some extent. Contemplate how deeply the person who hurt you must suffer to act the way they did. You are not condoning the behavior at this juncture but simply understanding the amount of deep suffering a person has to experience to behave so badly.

4. Share the compassion.
Breathe in compassion and love into your heart until this love and compassion is overflowing. Allow it to flow out where it needs to go, without effort on your part. Perhaps set the intention to allow this love and compassion to flow out to others who are suffering, including the person who hurt you.

5. Add in acceptance.
Continue to breathe love and compassion into your heart, and then begin to also breathe in acceptance. Breathe in and accept that you have been hurt and that you are also stronger as a result. Breathe in and accept that there is an abundance of hurt existing in the world. Breathe in and accept that you will not be another person that continues to spread hurt in the world.

6. Let it go.
Breathe the hurt all out. Breathe out and let go of everything you have been holding on to. Breathe out and let go of hurt, pain, suffering, your hold on the past, your worries about the future, your blame, shame, or anything else. Breathe out and release everything into freedom. All the while, breathe in love, compassion, and acceptance. Breathe out, setting the pain free into freedom.

7. Release and forgive.
Continue to breathe in love, compassion, and acceptance until your heart is again so full that the love, compassion, and acceptance begin to overflow from your heart without effort. When you begin to feel this love, compassion, and acceptance overflow your heart, imagine you are releasing the person who hurt you from your heart, body, and mind into freedom with forgiveness. You may wish to say this phrase as you do so: "I forgive you and release you into freedom."

You may wish to write about how you are feeling or about your experience.

When you release your own fears, anger, and negativity, as well as the suffering of others, into freedom, you find bliss. You are free. Free from binding thoughts, negativity, and suffering. You are free to be happy and joyful, as you were meant to be.

Epilogue
See Your Life as a Miracle

·······················

I remember the day my niece, Maia, was playing with her dolls, rolling them around in the dirt while giggling to herself. She must have been about four years old. The sun shone down on her so that the rays surrounded her like a halo, while the gentle breeze intermittently caused her curly hair to get in her face. At one point, she looked up and saw me gazing at her.

Curious, she asked me, "Auntie, why do you have that silly smile on your face?"

I answered, "I have a silly smile on my face because I am happy."

"Why are you happy?"

I answered, "I am happy because I am looking at a miracle."

She looked at me quizzically, head tilted. "What's a miracle?"

"A miracle is when something extraordinary and magnificent happens."

Maia tilted her head the other way as she thought about what I said. She scrunched her eyebrows up a bit as she tried to sum it all up.

Then she exclaimed, "Oh!" and started jumping up and down and dancing about as she shouted, "I'm a miracle! I'm a miracle!" She ran to her mother and grandmother shouting, "Hey Mom! Nona! I'm a miracle!" She ran to her grandfather exclaiming, "*Saaabbiii!!* I'm a miracle!"

Not only was this a sight to behold, but it also made me think. When is the last time I thought of myself as a miracle? When did children stop being told that they were miracles? If all of us in the world realized that we were miracles, would we suffer so much? Would we be so angry, fearful, and stressed?

If you think about it, it is pretty damn hard to be born. Getting conceived is challenging and passing through that birth canal, even harder. Managing to get as far as we have now, near impossible. It is really quite miraculous.

Don't you think?

See, if you were to awaken every day realizing that you were a miracle like Maia did, how bad of a mood would you be in? More than fixing your bad mood, believing in yourself as a miracle would enable you to believe in yourself as a powerful being who can overcome adversity to grow, learn, and forgive.

Does this mean believing you are a miracle translates to never getting angry? Unlikely. There will always be a situation that is unfair or a person who acts unkindly or unjustly that will cause anger to rise within you. Believing that you are a miracle simply gives you the bandwidth not to take situations personally and to be better able to problem solve, or grow from your problems. The better you feel about yourself, the less others or negative situations can take that feeling away from you. It doesn't mean you like negative situations or agree with bad behavior. It just means you aren't taking things to heart and have a better handle of seeing your way through. In other words, you are able to hold your balance, maintain your bliss, and maybe even spread that bliss to others rather than spreading more hurt and pain.

I urge you to complete this last exercise, one that is meant to remind you how incredibly valuable and wonderful you are, especially when you are down and out.

Epilogue Exercise: Superstar Miracle

- Kneel down on one knee while the other knee is bent and the foot is flat on the floor. Raise both arms to the sky.
- Scream as loud as you can, "I'm a miracle! I'm a miracle!"
- Stand up and do the superman pose as you state, "I'm a miracle! I'm a miracle!"
- Spin around and skip about and say in a sing-song voice, "I'm a miracle! I'm a miracle!"
- Take note of how you feel.
- Draw a picture of yourself in your power pose in this frame.

My Power Pose

Extra Charts

Distress Assessment Chart

What happened?	What is my physical reaction?	How is it making me feel?	How do I react?	What can I do to heal?	What is my new response?
Unsupported					
Ignored					
Rejection					
Humiliation					
Injustice					
Disappointment					
Grief/loss					
Illness/pain					

Distress Assessment Chart

What happened?	What is my physical reaction?	How is it making me feel?	How do I react?	What can I do to heal?	What is my new response?
Unsupported					
Ignored					
Rejection					
Humiliation					
Injustice					
Disappointment					
Grief/loss					
Illness/pain					

Nutrition/Mood Log

Food	Quantity	Time of day eaten	Time of symptom	Symptom and notes

Nutrition/Mood Log

Food	Quantity	Time of day eaten	Time of symptom	Symptom and notes

Activity/Mood Log

Day	Type of activity	Time of day	Mood before	Mood after
Monday				
Tuesday				
Wednesday				
Thursday				
Friday				
Saturday				
Sunday				

Activity/Mood Log

Day	Type of activity	Time of day	Mood before	Mood after
Monday				
Tuesday				
Wednesday				
Thursday				
Friday				
Saturday				
Sunday				

Soul Family Assessment Log

Relationship	Gives to me	Receives from me	Boosts my sense of Self	Hurts my sense of Self	My role in the dynamic
Mother					
Father					
Sibling					
Friend					
Coworker					

Soul Family Assessment Log

Relationship	Gives to me	Receives from me	Boosts my sense of Self	Hurts my sense of Self	My role in the dynamic
Mother					
Father					
Sibling					
Friend					
Coworker					

Sleep Assessment Log

Day	Hours slept night prior	Times waking up through night	Felt rested in a.m. (y/n)	Mood	Remarks
Monday					
Tuesday					
Wednesday					
Thursday					
Friday					
Saturday					
Sunday					

Sleep Assessment Log

Day	Hours slept night prior	Times waking up through night	Felt rested in a.m. (y/n)	Mood	Remarks
Monday					
Tuesday					
Wednesday					
Thursday					
Friday					
Saturday					
Sunday					

Power Chart

Negative feeling (label)	My role in it	Preferred feeling	Power to change	Power statement

Power Chart

Negative feeling (label)	My role in it	Preferred feeling	Power to change	Power statement

Notes

A Final Note from the Author

·······················

My hope for you is that this book has helped you find your bliss, even when your life isn't going as you planned. Always keep in mind that no matter the situation, you have a choice of how you proceed and whether you look at the situation through your victim lens or your superhero lens. Some days you will feel like a superhero and other days, not so much. It is up to you to make daily assessments as to what you can do to support yourself to be at your best.

Just as importantly, it is imperative that you learn to know and love yourself even when you are at your worst. The more you do so, the more likely that you will truly take care of yourself. It is when you are at your worst that you are the most depleted and the most in need of care. When you take care of yourself, you are less likely to get angry and blow up.

Always remember that bliss is not a far reach away. You always have the capacity to choose bliss, and now you have the tools to reach for it!

Acknowledgments

....

I first want to acknowledge my editor, Nicole Mele, for approaching me about writing this book. I am so grateful for being given the opportunity to share my knowledge and experience in such a delightful and accessible format.

I am also extremely grateful to the loves of my life who helped me learn to stand in love and use stress to my advantage. I am of course, thankful for my family: my mother and father, Shirley and Jacob Selhub; my siblings, Julie and Eliya Selhub; and my beautiful niece, Maia Selhub.

I have so many loves in my life that it is challenging to list all those who sparked my heart to find the compassion I needed to have for myself and others, but most of all, I want to thank my soul mates—Lisa Ross, Dorsey Schulman, Kimberly Wallace, Venita Bell Shaw, Sharon Freedman, Joe Smiddy, Chiara Piovella, Stasia Forsythe Sienna, Michael J. Gelb, Sylvia Frerk, and Beth Hogan Hamacher.

Lastly, thank you to all of my patients and clients who have been my greatest teachers.

References

1. a. Cannon, W. *The Wisdom of the Body*. New York: W.W. Norton & Company, 1963.

b. Cannon, W. *Bodily Changes in Pain, Hunger, Fear, and Rage*. New York: Appleton-Century-Crofts, 1929.

2. a. Selye, H. "Stress and disease." *Science*, October 1955, 122(3171): 625–631.

b. Fadel, Z., Johnson, S. K., Diamon, B. J., Zhanna, D., and Goolkasian, P. "Mindfulness meditation improves cognition: Evidence of brief mental training." *Consciousness and Cognition*, June 2010, 19(2): 597–605.

3. Kaptchuk, T. *The Web That Has No Weaver: Understanding Chinese Medicine*. New York: McGraw-Hill Education, 2000.

4. Selhub, E. *The Love Response: Your Prescription to Turn Off Fear, Anger, and Anxiety to Achieve Vibrant Health and Transform Your Life*. New York: Ballantine Books, 2009.

5. Lai, J. S., Hiles, S., Bisquera, A., Hure, A. J. McEvoy, M., and Attia, J. "A systematic review and meta-analysis of dietary patterns and depression in community-dwelling adults." *American Journal of Clinical Nutrition*, January 2014, 99(1): 181–197.

6. Warburton, D. E., Nicol, C. W., and Bredin, S. S. "Health benefits of physical activity: The evidence." *Canadian Medical Association Journal*, March 2006, 174(6): 801–809.

7. Uchino, B. N. "Social support and health: A review of physiological processes potentially underlying links to disease outcomes." *Journal of Behavioral Medicine*, August 2006, 29(4): 377–387.

8. Misra, S. and Stokols, D. "Psychological and health outcomes of perceived information overload." *Environment and Behavior,* November 2012, 44(6): 737–759.

9. Selhub, E. and Logan, A. *Your Brain on Nature.* Canada: HarperCollins, 2014.

10. Kawakami, K., Kawamoto, M., Nomura, M., Otani, H., Nabika, T., and Gonda, T. "Effects of phytoncides on blood pressure under restraint stress in SHRSP." *Clinical and Experimental Pharmacology and Physiology,* December 2004, Suppl 2: S27–28.

11. Beccuti, G., and Pannain, S. "Sleep and obesity." *Current Opinion in Clinical Nutrition and Metabolic Care,* July 2011, 14(4): 402–412.

12. Benson, H., and Klipper, M. Z. *The Relaxation Response.* New York: HarperTorch, First Avon Books, 1976.

13. Jacobs, G. D. "The physiology of mind-body interactions: The stress response and the relaxation response." *Journal of Alternative and Complementary Medicine,* 2001, 7(Suppl 1): S83–92.

14. Bhasin, M. K., Dusek, J. A., Chang, B-H., Joseph, M. G., Denninger, J. W., Fricchione, G. L., Benson, H., and Libermann, T. A. "Relaxation response induces temporal transcriptome changes in energy metabolism, insulin secretion and inflammatory pathways." *PLOS One,* May 2013, 8(5): e62817.

15. Davidson, R. J., Kabat-Zinn, J., Schumacher, J., Rosenkranz, M., Muller, D., Santorelli, S. F., Urbanowski, F., Harrington, A., Bonus, K., and Sheridan, J. F. "Alterations in brain and immune function produced by mindfulness meditation." *Psychosomatic Medicine,* July-August 2003, 65(4): 564–570.

16. Fadel, Z., Johnson, S. K., Diamond, B. J., David, Z., and Goolkasian, P. "Mindfulness meditation improves cognition: Evidence of brief mental training." *Consciousness and Cognition,* June 2010, 19(2): 597–605.

17. Praissman, S. "Mindfulness-based stress reduction: A literature review and clinician's guide." *Journal of the American Academy of Nursing Practitioners*, April 2008, 20(4): 212–216.

18. Kaptchuk, T. *The Web That Has No Weaver: Understanding Chinese Medicine.* New York: McGraw-Hill Education, 2000.

19. Fondin, M. "What is a chakra?" The Chopra Center, n.d. Retrieved from: https://chopra.com/articles/what-is-a-chakra#sm.0000276wkeibefaw11lng-0y4ala1x.

20. Carney, D. R., Cuddy, A. J. C., and Yap, A. J. "Power posing: Brief nonverbal displays affect neuroendocrine levels and risk tolerance." *Psychological Science*, September 2010, 21(10): 1363–1368.

21. Strean, W. B. "Laughter prescription." *Canadian Family Physician*, October 2009, 55(10): 965–967.

22. Kugler, L. and Kuhbandner, C. "That's not funny!—But it should be: Effects of humorous emotion regulation on emotional experience and memory." *Frontiers in Psychology*, August 2015, 6: 1296.

23. Edmonds, M. "What is laughter yoga?" How Stuff Works, n.d. Retrieved from: http://science.howstuffworks.com/life/laughter-yoga2.htm.

24. Carlsmith, K. M., Wilson, T. D., and Gilbert, D. T. "The paradoxical consequence of revenge." *Journal of Personality and Social Psychology*, 95(6): 1316–1324.

25. Hanh, T. N. *Anger: Wisdom for Cooling the Flames.* New York: Riverhead Books, 2001, pp. 91–92.

26. Toussaint, L. L., Worthington, E. L., and Williams, D. R. (Eds.). *Forgiveness and Health: Scientific Evidence and Theories Relating Forgiveness to Better Health.* Netherlands: Springer Netherlands, 2015.